SAMS
Teach Yourself

iMac

Rita Lewis

in 10 Minutes

SAMS

A Division of Macmillan Computer Publishing
201 West 103rd St., Indianapolis, Indiana, 46290 USA

SAMS TEACH YOURSELF
IMAC IN 10 MINUTES

Copyright © 1998 by Sams Publishing

International Standard Book Number: 0-672-31519-X

Library of Congress Catalog Card Number: 98-88376

Printed in the United States of America

First Printing: December 1998

00 99 98   4 3 2 1

EXECUTIVE EDITOR
Christopher Will

DEVELOPMENT EDITOR
Kate Shoup Welsh

MANAGING EDITOR
Brice Gosnell

PROJECT EDITOR
Kevin Laseau

COPY EDITOR
Pamela Woolf

INDEXER
Mary Gammons

TECHNICAL EDITOR
Lisa Lee

PROOFREADER
Benjamin Berg

LAYOUT TECHNICIAN
Marcia Deboy

TRADEMARKS

WARNING AND DISCLAIMER

CONTENTS

ABOUT THE AUTHOR

Rita Lewis is a freelance writer with over nine years of formal training in fine arts and design. She applied her MA in cultural anthropology to the observation of computer companies during her 10 years working as a proposal manager for various networking and mainframe organizations. In 1984, Rita fell in love with her first lowly Mac 512K and hasn't looked back. Rita is the author of over 10 books on various Macintosh topics, including collaborative authoring of the hardware sections of Hayden's *Maclopedia*, *Sams Teach Yourself Mac OS 8.5 in 24 Hours*, and *PageMill 2.0 Handbook*.

DEDICATION

To my family: Doug, Lisa, and Hannah.

ACKNOWLEDGMENTS

I would like to thank everyone at Sams for their quick wits and fast editing skills. I would especially like to acknowledge Chris Will, who has faith in my writing skills and patience with my child-rearing responsibilities; to Kate Welsh, who jumped in and ran with this book; to Kevin Laseau, who always makes my books happen; and to Lisa Lee, who always does such a superb job checking my facts.

TELL US WHAT YOU THINK!

As the reader of this book, *you* are our most important critic and commentator. We value your opinion and want to know what we're doing right, what we could do better, what areas you'd like to see us publish in, and any other words of wisdom you're willing to pass our way.

As the executive editor for the operating systems team at Macmillan Computer Publishing, I welcome your comments. You can fax, email, or write me directly to let me know what you did or didn't like about this book[md]as well as what we can do to make our books stronger.

Please note that I cannot help you with technical problems related to the topic of this book, and that due to the high volume of mail I receive, I might not be able to reply to every message.

When you write, please be sure to include this book's title and author, as well as your name and phone or fax number. I will carefully review your comments and share them with the author and editors who worked on the book.

Fax: 317-581-4663

Email: opsys@mcp.com

Mail: Executive Editor
            Operating Systems
            201 West 103rd Street
            Indianapolis, IN 46290 USA

INTRODUCTION TO iMAC

Welcome to the twenty first century. The Apple iMac is an innovative all-in-one Macintosh computer. This consumer computer really "thinks differently"—looking like it does with its pyramid-shaped bondi blue transluscent exterior and up-to-date interior components.

WHY THIS BOOK?

This book is perfect for the computer user who wants the basic facts about using an iMac without a lot of technical jargon.

- This book is broken down into 17 lessons, all easily read in 10 minutes or less. You don't have to spend a lot of time wading through long chapters and complicated explanations.

- This book focuses on the key things you have to know so that you can get comfortable using the iMac. You don't have to learn each and every little thing about Macintosh computers. By focusing on what you need to know, you can build your skills more easily.

- This book covers just about all main topics of using the iMac. You learn about hardware, networking, software, and the Macintosh OS 8.5 operating system. You learn the basic tasks for working with software as well as exploring the Internet. You learn how to work with the iMac's unique Universal Serial Bus (USB) ports and lack of a floppy drive, as well as how to make the most of the iMac's speed and ease of use. These are things you will use day after day. You might not need to learn too much more than what is covered here.

- This book contains lots of step-by-step instructions for common tasks. You can use these steps to learn how to perform these key tasks on the iMac. The step-by-step procedures are also illustrated with figures so that you know what you should see on your screen while you are trying out the tasks on the page.

Icons Used in this Book

In additon to the background information and step-by-step instructions, this book contains other useful tips, cautions, and notes, each identified with an icon.

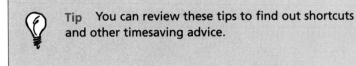

Tip You can review these tips to find out shortcuts and other timesaving advice.

Caution Read these cautions to avoid common mistakes and potential problems.

Plain English Read these notes to learn useful facts or additional information about the Mac OS and iMac.

Use this book as you explore the potentials of this great new computer. Have fun!

LESSON 1

WHAT IS AN iMAC?

In this lesson you will learn about the components of the iMac.

So you've just purchased this strange turquoise pyramid-shaped computer that looks like it comes from outer space: the iMac. *iMac* supposedly stands for *Internet Macintosh* because it has been optimized to work with the Internet. In reality, I think that it is just a jazzy name for a very radically different computer. Figure 1.1 shows you a rendering of the front of the iMac.

FIGURE **1.1**   The bondi-blue iMac is very different from other personal computers.

So what did you buy?

The iMac is an all-in-one computer harking back to the days in 1984 of the first Macintosh 128K. The iMac consists of the following, all in a single box:

- Macintosh computer

- High-resolution monitor

- Large hard drive

- CD-ROM drive

- High-fidelity stereo speakers

- 56Kbps internal modem

- An Apple USB standard 105-key keyboard

- A new round mouse

- IrDA-based infrared communications port

- 100Base-T Ethernet port

THE COMPUTER DEFINED

The iMac is a G3-based Macintosh computer powered by a 233MHz G3 PowerPC microprocessor. The *microprocessor* is the brains of the computer system. The microprocessor is the computer, residing on an integrated circuit board that, on the iMac, is conveniently located in a drawer at the bottom of the computer housing.

The computer housed on this logic board (also called a *motherboard*) is very advanced and very special. It is a reduced instruction set computer (*RISC*), meaning it contains a simplified set of instructions on a very fast chip set. By stringing together simplified instructions, RISC chips emulate their more populous complex instruction set computer (*CISC*) brethren— only faster, cooler, and more efficient. The PowerPC 750 used by the iMac and other high-end Apple Macintosh workstations and portable computers is also called the *G3* because it belongs to the third generation of PowerPC chips.

Like most modern Macintosh computers, the iMac bases its components on off-the-shelf technology. Three parts of the iMac are common PC components:

- Its RAM chips (SO-DIMMs)

- Its input/output ports (USB ports)

- The chips that assist the iMac in starting up

This makes it easy for you to upgrade memory, add-on cards, peripherals, and so forth.

RANDOM ACCESS MEMORY (RAM)

Every computer needs an area to store information while it is being processed; this area is called *random access memory* or *RAM*. The iMac's RAM is the same as the RAM used by Wintel personal computers. The iMac comes equipped with 32MB of RAM, but you can upgrade the iMac for a total 128MB of memory.

The iMac uses a secondary area of RAM on an ancillary circuit board (called a *daughter card*) termed *backside cache*, which stores instructions that can be used multiple times, thus speeding up processing by limiting the times that the computer has to wait for information to be transferred from storage.

> **Backside Cache**   The iMac comes with 512KB of backside cache. The backside cache is connected to the computer by a very fast 66MHz PCI system bus. Because the L2 cache bus is so fast, the iMac's 233MHz processor makes very good use of its L2 cache, thus enhancing its performance.

One downside of the iMac's chip configuration is that the iMac lacks an extra PCI slot, which negates the possibility of installing a popular gamer's board, the 3DFx accelerator chip. Only serious gaming users will worry about this negative issue, because the iMac does support the computational- and graphic-intensive nature of modern computer games. The upside is that the iMac does provide extensive support for such games as MacSoft's Quake, Bungie Software's Weekend Warrior, Activision's MechWarrior 2, and Pangea Software's Nanosaur (which comes bundled with the iMac).

THE MONITOR

One nice thing about the iMac is that it comes with a built-in 15-inch multisync monitor capable of providing resolutions of up to 1,024×768 pixels per inch. *Multisync* means that the monitor can display more than one resolution based on the pixel depth (number of colors) you want to display. The multisync monitor uses a built-in ATI IIc graphics chip set, which allows the iMac to accelerate the rendering of 2D and 3D images, making the iMac an excellent graphics computer.

All computer monitors, including the iMac's, display colors using three basic hues: red, green, and blue (also called RGB, which is why displays are sometimes termed RGB devices). Every color displayed on a monitor is derived from red, green, or blue phosphors. The iMac's monitor comes from the factory with a preset color profile (a set of colors it can accurately display). You can adjust this profile by using the ColorSync Monitor Calibration Assistant in the Monitors & Sound control panel. For more information about calibrating your iMac, see Chapter 11, "Color."

A *pixel* is the smallest possible area of screen that can be drawn. Color capabilities are generally given in *bits per pixel* measurements. Table 1.1 describes these pixel schemes.

TABLE 1.1   MONITOR PIXEL DEPTHS AND COLOR DISPLAY CAPABILITIES

PIXEL DEPTH	COLORS THAT CAN BE DISPLAYED
1-bit	2 (black and white)
2-bit	4
8-bit	256
16-bit	32,000
32-bit	16,000,000

The iMac's monitor provides a viewable screen size of 13.8 inches, which leaves a black border around the screen. The iMac monitor is capable of presenting several different screen resolutions based on the number of colors you want displayed (what is called *pixel depth*) and the amount of video RAM (called *SGRAM*) you have installed. Table 1.2 presents a list of possible resolutions and their color capabilities.

TABLE 1.2 iMac Screen Resolution and Color Capabilities

Resolution	Refresh Rate	Pixel Depth
640×480	117Hz	32-bit (millions of colors)
800×600	95Hz	32-bit (millions of colors)
1,024×768	75Hz	16-bit (thousands of colors)

HARD DISKS, FLOPPY, AND CD-ROM DRIVES

The iMac's CD-ROM drive is very rudimentary, lacking a CD tray and exposing the guts of the system to the outside whenever you open its drawer. At first look, it is difficult to figure out how to insert a CD into the iMac, but here's what you do:

1. Manually press the center circle of the CD onto the drive's ring until you hear a snap.

2. Gently tuck the disc into the player and close the drawer.

> **Play Some Music**   You can play audio CDs on your iMac, and the sound quality is really great! Insert a CD into the drive bay, and then use the AppleCD Audio Player on the Apple menu to manage the sound quality and playability of audio CDs.

The iMac does not come with a floppy drive—a point that is driven home by every reviewer. You can install a removable cartridge drive made by Imation that supports both existing 1.4MB floppies as well as 120MB removable disks. Other vendors will be offering similar USB-based products soon.

The lack of a floppy drive makes it difficult to install older floppy-based software, to share files with PC users when you are not connected to a network, or to save small files outside your iMac. To replace this seeming lack, try using the Internet, the iMac's infrared communications capability, or removable disks.

> **Need a Virtual Floppy?** A new service on the Internet offers a virtual floppy for iMac users for free. The site, found at http://imacfloppy.com, offers 4MB of free space to iMac users. This space can be used to exchange files over the Internet with other users, no matter which platform they currently work on. Other entrepreneurs might also get into this act.

THE MULTIMEDIA SYSTEM

The iMac provides a complete multimedia system, including a built-in microphone, 16-bit stereo speakers, sound input and output jacks, and SRS (sound retrieval system), providing enhanced quality sound.

The following audio ports are provided:

- A built-in microphone and microphone port. If you insert an external microphone, such as Apple's PlainTalk mic; the built-in mic is automatically muted.

- An external stereo sound input jack.

- An internal sound system supporting the CD player.

The iMac sound system sends sounds to built-in speakers, the sound output jack, and two headphone jacks placed on the front of the iMac housing. The SRS 3D system can be manually adjusted to fit your listening needs via the Monitors & Sounds control panel's Sound screen.

COMMUNICATIONS

The iMac includes an internal Hayes-compatible hardware modem that provides connections at 56K baud. The modem is used with the Open Transport/PPP and AppleTalk Remote Access software that comes with the Mac OS 8.1 system. Note that you must have a special file called iMac Internal 56k CCL installed in your System Folder in order to be able to run the modem.

The iMac also includes an infrared communications port that can automatically detect IrDA-based communications from other infrared-equipped computers, such as the PalmPilot or Apple G3 PowerBook portable computer. The infrared transmitter/receiver is located behind a dark red plastic cover on the front of the iMac. The infrared lens transmits infrared light in a 30-degree radius, pointing outward from the computer. The recommended minimum distance between devices is three feet. IrDA supports transmission rates of 4MB/second and can use both AppleTalk and TCP/IP protocols.

The iMac also provides both 10BaseT (thinnet) and 100BaseT (thicknet) Ethernet support on its main logical board. Both types of Ethernet connections use the same port, allowing the iMac do the speed detection and automatically accommodate as necessary. All you have to do is configure the TCP/IP control panel to recognize Ethernet and the AppleTalk control panel to accept Remote Access Only, and the iMac will function fully on an Ethernet-based network.

THE KEYBOARD AND MOUSE

The iMac's keyboard and mouse are no longer connected to the Mac by an Apple Desktop bus, but rather by a USB bus just like all other peripherals. The keyboard is a PC-standard keyboard with slightly different key arrangement than what Mac users are used to (the arrangement is very familiar to PC users).

The mouse is very new and peculiar. It may take you a while to get used to the roundness of it, but it is great for small hands that cannot get a proper grip on the standard ADB mouse.

In this chapter, you learned about the components of the iMac, including the monitor, the hard disk, the CD-ROM drive, the multimedia system, the communications system, and the keyboard and mouse.

LESSON 2

THE MAC OPERATING SYSTEM

In this lesson you will learn about the Mac OS 8.5 interface and explore its various multimedia tools. You will also learn how to use iMac to browse the Internet.

The operating system is the engine that runs the computer. In the iMac, the operating system is split between hardware and software with portions located on Read Only Memory (ROM) chips and large amounts located in the System Folder. The current operating system version is Mac OS 8.5, although due to the timing of the iMac introduction, the first iMacs were bundled with an upgraded version of Mac OS 8.1.

iMac OS 8.1 integrates advanced Internet access features such as the built-in Internet Config application (called *Internet*) and the Apple Remote Access 3.0 application present in Mac OS 8.5. This book describes Mac OS 8.5 because by the time you read this, most iMacs will be shipping with this operating system.

WORKING WITH THE MAC OS 8.5 GUI

The place where you work with files and disks on the iMac is called the desktop; it is the creation of an application called the Finder. The Finder is responsible for managing files, providing easy access via folders and windows, dialog boxes, and a universal series of commands for opening, closing, saving, and printing that is available in every application you use on the iMac.

Finder 8.5 is the current version of the Finder. The first obvious change to Finder 8.5 is the appearance of icons, folders, and Finder menus (see Figure 2.1). The three-dimensional platinum windows, sliders, and buttons make it easier to understand what each window tool does, whether snapping open the window, closing the window, resizing a window, or scrolling through a window. You can set up how you view your windows and folders; you can view them as icons or set them up as easier-to-read lists. In addition, you can create your own filing system by dragging selected folders onto the bottom of your desktop. When you drag any open folder window to the bottom of your window, these windows turn into little tabs that you can click to spring the contents of that folder open or shut. These neat tabs also are drag sensitive. Drag an item over the tab to see the window pop open to receive the item. You can also move the pop-up window along the bottom of the desktop.

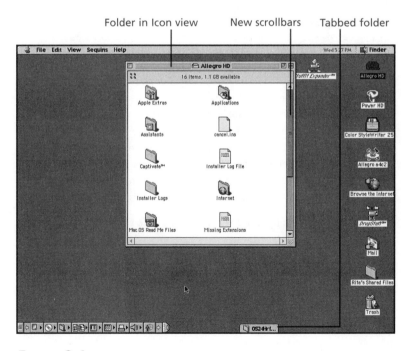

FIGURE 2.1   The iMac desktop.

EXPLORING MAC OS 8.5 MULTIMEDIA TOOLS

The iMac comes with an extensive array of multimedia tools. This software consists of several technologies, including the following:

- QuickTime

- QuickTime VR

- QuickDraw 3D

These technologies hide behind the scenes until you need them for the seamless display and manipulation of three-dimensional spaces and objects, as well as for the painless display of audio and video documents.

QUICKTIME 3.0

QuickTime 3.0 is Apple's technology that lets your computer play audio and video movie files either directly on your iMac via the new MoviePlayer and PictureViewer components or over the Internet via the updated QuickTime browser plug-in. Although this technology looks deceptively simple, together MoviePlayer and PictureViewer represent over 175 different software features. These software components can be combined into about 20 categories of services relating to multimedia, which Apple developers add to their products. What this all means is that QuickTime 3.0 brings a wealth of multimedia features to Mac OS 8.5 and to Macintosh multimedia hardware and software products.

QuickTime 3.0 has many new features you can use to view many diverse audio and video formats without worrying about what type of file format you are attempting to view. QuickTime's vast array of support tools include the MPEG1 extension, which was introduced with QuickTime 2.5. It lets you play back MPEG1-formatted files with applications such as MoviePlayer 2.5 (see Figure 2.2).

QUICKTIME VR

QuickTime VR is Apple's virtual reality technology, which turns a series of photos into a virtual reality world (see Figure 2.3). If, for example, you navigate a QuickTime VR file, you can navigate inside a room, with the capability to turn full-circle in the room and zoom toward or away from the visual elements contained in that room. QuickTime VR files can be created with special virtual reality cameras or purely with software-based images such as 3D worlds. Mac OS 8.5 installs QuickTime VR 2.0 along with QuickTime software.

FIGURE 2.2   QuickTime MoviePlayer.

FIGURE 2.3   QuickTime VR.

QUICKDRAW 3D

As its name denotes, QuickDraw 3D is Apple's 3D technology (see Figure 2.4). Its API libraries support interactive rendering, 3D interface features, and the industry-standard 3DMF file format. QuickDraw 3D supports any application that uses this technology, plus the iMac's built-in ATI Rage IIc 3D graphics hardware.

FIGURE 2.4   QuickDraw 3D and SimpleText.

BROWSING THE INTERNET

Mac OS 8.5 includes a built-in manager for the various control panel settings you need to access the Internet. This control panel, called Internet, provides the same configuration support once provided by the Internet Config shareware product. Here, in one handy place, is a way to manage all the myriad pieces of software required to connect you successfully to the Internet, including your browser, PPP connection, TCP/IP software, and modem hardware and software.

The iMac desktop lets you reach the Internet in several ways: via a Browser button, a Data Detector contextual menu, an Email button, an Apple menu item, and various AppleScript items. All these enhancements build on the OpenTransport technologies that lie under the Mac OS 8.5 hood.

In addition, Apple has added two more Internet tools to Mac OS 8.5: Macintosh Runtime Java support and a Personal Web server. You have the choice to use either the default Microsoft Internet Explorer browser or Netscape's Navigator browser, because both are included with the iMac.

iMac provides the following Internet and Internet-related software.

- Microsoft Internet Explorer 4—Microsoft's popular Web browser application is installed as your default browser in the Internet folder at the root level of the hard disk.

- Internet control panel—A useful utility that generates a universal Internet configuration across all your various Internet software so that you can easily switch between email programs or browsers without having to change your email address, news address, or home page designation.

- Apple Remote Access (ARA) formerly Open Transport/PPP—Point-of-presence software used for dialing in to the Internet or other network from outside. ARA provides a dialer, Status dialog box, control strip component, and control panel for managing the connection to your Internet service provider (ISP).

- StuffIt Expander—Allows you to expand compressed files downloaded from the Internet.

- DropStuff Expander—Lets you expand a compressed file by dropping it over this application's icon. StuffIt Expander and DropStuff Expander are both standard Mac file decompression applications published by Aladdin.

- Internet Setup Assistant—Allows you to configure all iMac's network settings, including registering with an ISP, without having to open any control panels.

- Acrobat Reader 3.0—An application that can read PDF files. A set of fonts plus the Acrobat application and PDF file creator for Chooser are part of this software installation.

- HTML and Apple Guide support files—Files installed with Apple's Internet software that provide general information and support for the installed software.

PERSONAL WEB SERVER

Licensed from Maxum, Web Sharing works with Apple's File Sharing technology to turn your iMac into a personal miniaturized Web server (see Figure 2.5). Web Sharing allows you to publish documents and HTML-based pages on the Internet from your iMac (albeit to a small group of connected Macs because the bandwidth opening to your iMac is very small when using Personal Web Sharing). It also lets you manage uploading and downloading tasks on Web server's FTP server. The software adds

a Web Sharing control panel, sets your iMac's Web identity, such as the
location of your HTML files, and lets you turn Web Sharing on or off
with some general access privileges.

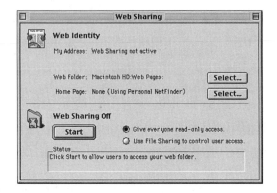

FIGURE 2.5   The Web Sharing control panel.

INTRODUCING THE NEW EXTENDED FILE SYSTEM

Every version of the Macintosh operating system up until now has been
based on a filing system, called the *Standard Format*, which allocates
64KB of disk space no matter how large a file actually is. In addition, you
probably didn't realize it, but your old Mac had a limit to the number of
files that can be stored on its hard drive. Mac OS 8 introduces the
Extended Format file system (also called *Hierarchical Filing System Plus*
or *HFS+*). You can format your hard disks or removable disks as
Extended Format disks, thus optimizing the storage capacity of today's
large multi-gigabyte hard disks by allocating the actual disk space
required to store a file. An added benefit is that you now can save more
than 65,000 files on your hard disk. The Extended Format is intended for
hard disks of 1GB or greater.

In this lesson, you learned about the Mac OS 8.5 interface, and you
explored Mac OS 8.5 multimedia tools. You also learned about using your
iMac to browse the Internet, and you were introduced to the new
Extended Format file system.

LESSON 3

ADD-ONS: EXTRA HARDWARE

In this lesson you will learn about add-on hardware, including USB adapters, hubs, and cables. You will also explore storage options.

A lot has been written about the dearth of hardware available for the iMac. The fact is, these writers have yet to change their mind-set away from serial, SCSI, and ADB ports toward the new (for Mac) universal serial bus port technology. Apple is converting its computers to this industry standard because USB provides the following benefits:

- *Hot-plugability*—USB peripherals can be installed on the iMac without the need to turn off the computer. This gives you the chance to change peripherals on-the-fly. For example, you can unplug a removable drive and plug in a scanner without stopping your work.

- *Easy installation*—USB peripherals use device drivers that are dynamically loaded by the system whenever it senses the presence of the device. Just drag and drop the driver onto the System Folder or run an installer.

- *Connectivity*—USB ports and peripherals do not require ID numbers, addresses, or terminators. In addition, USB cables come in only one flavor: USB A-B.

  USB cables have other advantages, as well. For example, USB cables have a female connector on one end and a male on the other, making their connection easy to figure out. Also, USB cables can be extended up to 5 meters, but most cables come in 2-, 3- and 5-meter lengths.

  There are two types of USB cables:

- Low-speed cables that are unshielded with non-twisted conductors used to transmit data at 1.5Mbps for 3 meters to a device they are soldered to, such as a mouse or keyboard.

- High-speed cables composed of two shielded twisted-pair wires. These high-speed cables are "fully rated" to transmit data at the USB maximum speed of 12Mbps.

- *Expandability*—USB supports the simultaneous connection of up to 127 devices to a single USB port through the use of hubs. Each of the two USB ports on the iMac connects four to seven peripherals or additional hubs. For example, the keyboard is a hub connecting the mouse and another peripheral, such as scanner or camera or an additional hub.

- *Excellent Performance*—The USB ports provide from 1.5Mbps up to 12Mbps data exchange rates. This speed can best be compared to the Apple desktop bus that provided speeds of 10Kbps and standard serial ports that provided speeds of 230Kbps.

USB thus provides many advantages over traditional SCSI and serial connectivity options. The thing to remember about the iMac is that the ports shown in Table 3.1 are no longer available (the table lists iMac equivalents for each defunct port).

TABLE 3.1   IMAC CONNECTION OPTIONS

DEFUNCT PORTS	USES	CONNECTIVITY OPTION
Apple desktop bus	Mouse, keyboard, joysticks, tablets	USB to ADB adapter
Serial ports (RS-232/RS-422 connectors)	Printers, scanners, modems	USB to serial adapter
SCSI	External hard drives, removable hard drives, CD-ROM, video cameras, and so on	USB ports

DEFUNCT PORTS	USES	CONNECTIVITY OPTION
Parallel	PC printers, scanners, and so on	USB to parallel adapter

USB ADAPTERS, HUBS, AND CABLES

One of the benefits of using USB is the capability to link peripherals to your iMac in groups of four to seven devices. USB uses hubs or groupings of ports to connect devices. You do not need to use a hub if you have fewer than three devices to connect, because USB peripherals can be plugged in and out without turning off the iMac.

There are two types of hubs:

- *Bus-powered hubs* (also called *passive hubs*)   Hubs that take their power directly from the cable that connects them to the iMac (or another hub). No two bus-powered hubs can be connected directly together because the hub farthest away from the power source at the iMac might not be capable of providing the minimum power required for the hub's ports. Alternate a bus-powered hub with a self-powered hub when linking hubs "downstream" from the iMac.

- *Self-powered hubs* (also called *active hubs*)   Hubs that contain their own AC adapter–based power supply. Because these hubs do not require power from the iMac, they can be used in any position on a system of daisy-chained hubs.

Hubs can be included in other hardware devices, such as displays, keyboards, and printers. In fact, the iMac's keyboard is a hub containing two additional ports. Such devices are called *compound devices*. You can use hubs to attach USB devices or legacy devices to your iMac. In order to attach serial, ADB, or parallel port devices, you need to purchase an adapter cable. Adapters change the signals from one set of wiring configurations to another.

There are four types of adapters available for use in attaching legacy peripherals to your iMac:

- USB-to-serial adapters

- USB-to-ADB adapters

- USB-to-parallel adapters

- LocalTalk-to-Ethernet adapters

 **Attaching SCSI Devices** As of the printing of this book, there is no way to attach small computer serial interface (SCSI) devices, such as hard drives, removables, or CD-ROM drives to your iMac. One company, Formac, is developing a USB-to-SCSI adapter card called iPower RAID, which is supposed to be available by late 1998 for a price of $150.

Tables 3.2 and 3.3 list the hubs, cables, and adapters announced as of this book's printing.

TABLE 3.2   HUBS

VENDOR	PRICE/AVAILABILITY	DESCRIPTION
Peracom	$79/Immediate	USB Quad hub. 4-port hub with power supply and USB cable
Entrega	$79.95/Immediate	USB hub. 4-port on back panel with power supply
Entrega	$129.95/Immediate	USB hub. 7-port on back panel with power supply
Belkin	Immediate	ExpressBus, 4-port passive hub
Farallon	Immediate	Starlet Ethernet hub. 10Base-T Ethernet expander
Inside Out	$199/Immediate	Hubport/7. 7-port active hub

TABLE 3.3   ADAPTERS AND CABLE

Vendor	Price/Availability	Description
Farallon	$99/Immediate	Two types of EtherMac iPrint Adapters: SL for connecting serial-port inkjet printers without LocalTalk to iMacs; LT for connecting printers with LocalTalk to iMacs.
Epson	$49.95/Immediate	USB/parallel printer adapter. Connects Epson Stylus photo and color printers to iMac. Includes adapter and drivers.
Hewlett-Packard	$69/Immediate	Printer cable kit. Connect HP Deskjet 670 series, 690 series. Includes adapter and drivers.
ALPS	Late 1998	MD-1300. Connect to Micro Dry dye sublimation printers.
Sonic Systems	Immediate	MicroPrint and MicroBridge. Pocket-sized LocalTalk to Ethernet hardware bridges. Lets 2 to 12 LocalTalk devices attach to iMac. Pocket-sized TCP/IP to Ethernet bridge.
Asante	Immediate	Micro AsantePrint. LocalTalk-to-Ethernet bridge supporting up to eight devices, including other Macs.
InfoWave	$99/Immediate	PowerPrint USB-to-parallel adapter. Lets iMac print

continues

TABLE 3.3   CONTINUED

VENDOR	PRICE/AVAILABILITY	DESCRIPTION
		from parallel-port based printers. Includes drivers and cable.
Apple		StyleWriter EtherTalk adapter. Connects Apple StyleWriter inkjet printers to iMac via the Ethernet port.
Griffin	$60/Late 1998	iPort adapter. Adapter card fits into mezzanine or perch slot where removable plate is located on iMac's side. Device supports video out, serial devices, including MIDI, bar code readers, wand scanners, tablets, lab equipment, modems, and cameras.

STORAGE OPTIONS

Because the iMac does not include a floppy drive, transporting data from Macs to PCs or other non-networked computers is difficult. This also makes installing legacy software that does not come on CD-ROMs difficult. In addition, backing up small files becomes a chore, but it is not impossible to overcome this shortcoming.

There are several ways to transfer data between computers that do not entail hooking up a peripheral device:

- *Use the Internet*—The best way is to upload the data to an FTP site on the Internet, and then download it to the iMac. Use your browser or a specialized FTP application such as Fetch 3.03 and enter the URL of the FTP site and your email address as a password. Check with the Webmaster for security issues before dialing in to the FTP site. If the file is small enough (under 1MB), you can email it to yourself from another computer and open it on the iMac.

* *Use a virtual floppy*—Make use of a new site on the Web (www.imacfloppy.com) that offers free 4MB of storage area for saving and transferring data to and from iMacs.

* *Transmit the data*—You can use the infrared communications capability of your G3 PowerBook to transmit your data to the iMac's IrDA receiver.

* *Set up a network*—You can connect another Mac to the iMac using a LocalTalk-to-Ethernet bridge and file sharing (see Chapter 14, "File Sharing," and Chapter 16, "Talking to the Other Guys," for more information).

The iMac also does not support SCSI devices, so the question becomes, how do you transfer all the data you have accumulated on external hard drives onto drives that are supported by the iMac? The easiest way is to connect the iMac to another Mac that uses the SCSI device and use File Sharing to transfer the data. If you are connected to a network via Ethernet, there is no problem, because the iMac plugs directly into an Ethernet network. If you are running a LocalTalk network, purchase one of the LocalTalk-to-Ethernet bridge adapters listed in Table 3.3 to connect the iMac to other Macs. File sharing lets you mount the SCSI onto the iMac's desktop, where you can use it as if it was a local volume.

The other solution is to copy all the data to one of the following USB storage devices:

* *Imation USB SuperDisk*—This removable disk drive stores up to 120MB of data but can also read standard 1.4MB floppy disks (both Mac and PC-formatted) for $149.99. The device was jointly developed by Panasonic and Imation and uses special LS-120 SuperDisk disks.

* *SyQuest SparQ*—1GB removable cartridge hard drive for $199 with availability at Christmas shopping season. These drives are slower than other removables (at a data transfer rate of 0.7MBs per second) but faster than standard floppy disk drives.

- *Newer Technology iDrive Floppy*—Another USB floppy disk drive; $90. Availability late fourth quarter, 1998.

- *Iomega Zip drive*—100MB Zip drive that is compatible with other Zips but operates with USB. Priced at $149 with availability late fourth quarter, 1998.

- *LaCie hard drives*—2.1, 4.5, and 8.4GB drives on USB-based hard drives for Windows 98 or iMacs.

FOR MORE INFORMATION

There is an increasing amount of great information about working with legacy systems on the iMac on the Internet. Here are some of the better Web sites:

- Apple's iMac site (`www.apple.com/imac/`) offers an extensive array of excellent information about USB peripherals, troubleshooting, and general iMac information.

- ImacinTouch (`www.macintouch.com/imacusb.html`) by Rick Ford of *MacWeek* fame offers up-to-date information about iMac peripherals, availability, news, software updates, and USB devices.

- MacWorld's iMac site called iMacworld (`www.imacworld.com`) is part of a Web ring of great iMac sites. This site provides news, icons, screen shots, videos, troubleshooting guides, reviews, USB device announcements, benchmarks, and many more sources of accurate information about iMac.

- The Mining Company's iMac site (`www.macsupport.miningco.com/blcenter.htm`) offers links to hundreds of Mac support sites including iMac information and USB information. A one-stop shopping center.

In this lesson you learned about add-on hardware, including USB adapters, hubs, and cables. You also explored storage options.

Lesson 4

Setting Up the iMac

In this lesson you will learn how easy it is to set up your iMac.

Having only three mandatory connections, the iMac was designed to be set up rapidly and used in an office or home environment. The iMac has a very small footprint, and is relatively lightweight (it even offers a handle on the top for easy carrying!). The use of USB ports makes plugging in peripherals very foolproof. One I/O access area, called the *mezzanine*, provides access to all the cables you need.

Plugging in the Keyboard

The iMac keyboard is slightly different from a standard Mac keyboard in several ways. The most basic way is that the Power On/Off switch is located on the top-right rim of the keyboard. It does not light up when the iMac is on. Notice that the keyboard is slightly smaller than other Mac keyboards and might take some getting used to because it is more ergonomically designed than older keyboards (for example, it lacks legs and slants slightly downward to help prevent repetitive stress disorder).

The keyboard that comes with the iMac is a USB passive hub containing two ports. Use one of the ports to connect the mouse (either on the right or left, depending on which hand you use) and use the other port to connect another hub, joysticks, tablets, scanners, lab equipment, and so forth. The keyboard plugs into one of the USB ports on the side of the iMac.

1. Open the I/O access plate (the plastic door on the right side of the iMac) by carefully pulling on the cable hole.

2. As shown in Figure 4.1, select a port (they are numbered Port 1 and Port 2 so that you can easily identify the location of your peripherals).

Pick Either One   The USB ports share the same controller, so it doesn't matter which one you select.

Type A ports
(USB)

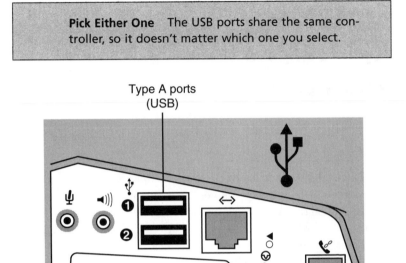

Universal Serial Bus (USB)

FIGURE 4.1   Plug the Type A connector into the USB port.

3. Plug the keyboard's USB cable's connector into the port through
   the cable hole.

There are two types of USB connectors:

• *Type A* connectors are used to connect devices to USB hubs.
  Anything that contains a USB port is considered a *hub*. The
  iMac is a hub and contains two Type A USB ports. Type A connectors have a middle plastic rim offset to one side.

• *Type B* connectors are used to connect to the USB device. Often
  this end is soldered to the device. Type B connectors are the
  smaller and narrower of the two types of connectors.

Type A and B connectors can be inserted only one way, and they lock in
place when correctly inserted. USB cables come with a Type A side and a
Type B side.

Be Careful!   Any USB device connected to the keyboard hub's USB port must be either a self-powered active hub or a low-power device.

PLUGGING IN THE MOUSE

Plug the mouse's Type A connector into the right or left side of the keyboard, depending on which hand you want to use.

PLUGGING IN THE MODEM

The iMac contains a 56K baud internal Hayes-compatible modem. The modem's port is located in the I/O access panel. Take the telephone cable (RS-232 connector) and feed it through the cable hole and plug it into the modem port shown in Figure 4.1. Plug the other side of the telephone cable into the telephone jack in the wall.

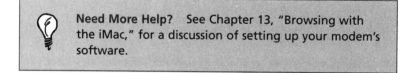
Need More Help?   See Chapter 13, "Browsing with the iMac," for a discussion of setting up your modem's software.

PLUGGING IN THE POWER

Plug the power cable into the power port to the right of the I/O access panel (refer to Figure 4.1). It is recommended that you not plug the power plug directly into the wall. Purchase a surge protector—such as one made by Kensington—for about $50 and plug all your power supplies into this protection device.

You have now set up your iMac and are ready to go.

In this lesson, you learned that setting up your iMac is a snap. You learned how to plug in your keyboard, mouse, modem, and power.

LESSON 5
GETTING
ORIENTED

In this lesson you will learn how to maneuver through iMac using the desktop, windows, menus folder, and files. You will also learn how to eject discs, use the Trash Can, and start up and shut down your iMac.

The desktop is the heart and soul of the iMac. Here you will find icons representing your hard disks, networked volumes, browsing tools, aliases to regularly used applications, the default printer, the Trash Can, and the menu bar that lets you access the contents of your iMac. You will quickly learn how to interpret the behavior of windows, icons, dialog boxes, menus, and aliases so that you can read the status of your iMac at a glance. The secret is that it is all done with pictures.

THE DESKTOP

The Desktop is similar to other windows in the Finder; however, it cannot be closed (except if the iMac is accessed over the network). You can only view items in Icon mode in the desktop window, which is the most convenient place to store files, or aliases to folders or files, that you frequently use.

The desktop (see Figure 5.1) consists of four main areas that are all generated by the Finder. These areas are the Finder's menu bar, Hard Drive icon (also called a *volume*), Trash Can icon, and desktop window (the desktop). From these areas you can access everything from software applications to the Internet.

iMac is a very versatile machine because it offers many different ways to perform your work. All these methods work because the iMac's icons always operate the same way, no matter where you are working: on the desktop, in a window, or in an application. For example, you are given more than four ways to open documents on your iMac:

- You can select an icon, click and hold down the mouse on a menu bar, and then drag the cursor down to select a command, such as **Open** on the **File** menu.

- You can press a keyboard equivalent, such as ⌘+O for Open.

- You can double-click one of the little pictures (called *icons*) to open its associated file (either an application or its related document).

- You can select a document's icon and drag it on top of an application icon or its alias.

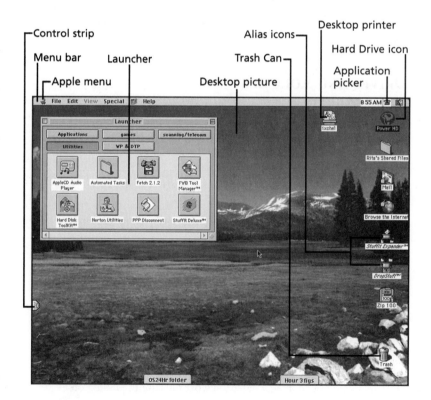

FIGURE 5.1 The iMac desktop.

Let's look more closely at the desktop's main components.

THE MENU BAR

The menu bar provides access to many software components of iMac and also monitors which applications are working with iMac. On the left end of the menu bar is the Apple menu. It consists of small programs called desk accessories, such as the Chooser and Key Caps, the Note Pad, and Stickies; as well as aliases to important folders and applications such as Control Panels, Chooser, Recent Applications, and so forth. On the right end of the menu bar is the Application menu. This menu contains a list of all currently open applications that are running on iMac. The Finder appears in this menu, as will any other open applications. The other menus (File, Edit, View, Special, and Help) provide commands that let you customize your iMac experience as well as open, print, save, copy, cut, paste, and view your iMac's contents in many different ways.

DRIVES AND VOLUMES

The Hard Drive icon represents the internal hard drive in your iMac. Typically, this icon also represents your Startup disk (the hard drive containing your active System Folder). The Startup disk's icon always appears at the very top of the stack of icons on your desktop.

> **Tip**   From now on, when I omit the word icon from these discussions and write Startup disk or window, you can assume that I mean their iconic representations.

Double-clicking the Hard Drive opens a window that represents the *root*, or base level, of items on the hard drive. If you have other drives, such as Zip drives or other external drives, they will also appear as icons on the desktop. In addition, if you are connected to a network, you might see an icon representing the network volume. You work with network volumes in the same manner you do any other local hard disk after you log on to them using the Chooser.

The Trash Can

You can delete as many files and folders as you like by using the Trash
Can icon located at the lower-right corner of your iMac's desktop. When
the Trash Can has one or more items in it, its icon changes to a "full"
Trash Can. You can empty the Trash Can by selecting Empty Trash from
the Special menu.

Using the Windows and Menus

The first thing you see on your iMac is that everything looks three-dimensional. (Apple calls this the *Platinum Appearance.*) Windows stand out,
the Trash Can has a shadow, and folders stand up. There is a method to
this elegance. The 3D appearance provides visual cues as to where you
are. The *active window* (meaning the window currently selected) appears
three-dimensional, as shown in Figure 5.2. Click an inactive window, and
it bounces to the front and changes its appearance. New controls on the
window let you manipulate it with fewer mouse clicks.

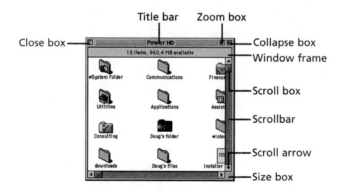

Figure 5.2   iMac windows provide elegant controls.

iMac introduces some innovative window behavior that proves very help-
ful when you want to move files and folders around without using extra
mouse clicks. iMac's windows spring, pop, and scroll by themselves.

MANIPULATING FILES AND FOLDERS

Everything on iMac is either a file or a folder. Folders open to reveal windows containing other files and folders (you can nest them inside each other ad infinitum). Figure 5.3 illustrates how files and folders can be nested.

FIGURE 5.3   You can nest folders within folders, thus creating a pyramid filing system.

Files and folders are easily created, but can become difficult to locate and organize. The iMac provides several ways to manage the deluge of folders that can swamp your desktop. The View menu with its View Options command, the Edit menu's Preferences command, and the General Controls control panel let you set how files and folders are displayed: whether as icons, buttons on a bar, lists, or whether in a staggered or straight alignment. You can also color-label the importance of files and folders, determine how icons are displayed, and much more.

THE FOLDER WINDOW

The Folder window is the second most basic feature of the iMac. It contains controls to open, close, window shade, enlarge, and move through the window to get where you want to be. Figure 5.4 presents a generic folder window and identifies its components.

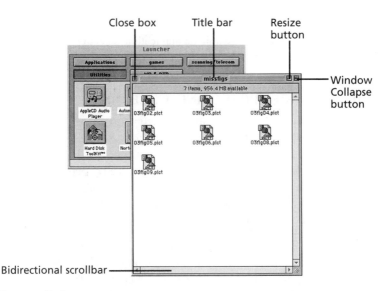

FIGURE 5.4   The Folder window.

There are many ways to select items in a folder window after it is open:
The easiest way is to click the item to be opened. However, if the item is
not immediately visible, you can use the scrollbars to navigate up, down,
left, or right around the window. The tab and arrow keys can also scroll
through the contents of a window. If the name of the item to be found is
known, you can type its name, and the Finder will reposition the window
to show you that particular file or folder.

CREATING FILES AND FOLDERS

You can create a folder in any Finder window by selecting New in the
Finder's File menu (or by pressing the keyboard combination ⌘+N. You
can name a file or folder by selecting an item and pressing Return. This
highlights the name of the file or folder, enabling you to rename it with a
name containing up to 32 characters. You can get information on any file
or folder by selecting General Information or Sharing Information from
the Get Info submenu of the File menu or by pressing ⌘+I.

Files are created by applications. You can create a new file by selecting
New from the application's File menu. First, enter some text then select

Save ⌘+S from the File menu. The file is created on your iMac's hard drive. To open the file from within an application, select Open from the File menu or press ⌘+O.

MOVING AND PROTECTING FOLDERS

To prevent some files and folders from being moved around unnecessarily, you can protect your System and Application folders from losing their content. Go to the General Controls control panel in the Control Panels pull-down menu on the Apple menu and activate the protection check boxes for either the System or Application folder (or both). If someone attempts to move a file or folder out of these folders (located at the root level of the hard drive), the Finder shows an alert and does not allow it.

You can move files and folders by selecting one or several and dragging them to any other window, folder, or to the desktop. You drag items by clicking them while holding down the mouse button, and then moving that item around a window or onto the desktop. If you drag a file onto a window from another hard drive, or a window or folder from a server, the Finder copies those items to that drive (provided there is enough room, or you have the adequate privileges on the server). When files or folders are copied, the originals remain on the source hard drive.

STARTING UP AND SHUTTING DOWN

Turning your iMac on and off is as easy as pressing a button. In fact, to start up your iMac that is all you do: Press the Power button on the iMac's front. When you press the Power button to start up the iMac, you get that old smiley face on your screen as the iMac commences its startup checks.

Shutting down is slightly more complicated. There are two ways to shut down:

- Turning off your computer hardware (called *Shut down*). You should always shut down before you completely turn off the machine.

- Restarting the iMac's software without powering down (called *Restart*).

The iMac lacks a Power key on its keyboard. Always select the **Shutdown** or Restart commands from the **Special** menu to turn off the iMac. The iMac does have a Programmer's Reset switch in its ports outlet. Reach around the side, open the little door, and carefully press a recessed button labeled Reset. The iMac will restart. Note that this is a drastic way to restart because it does not allow the computer to properly put away its open files.

Whenever you shut down, you are given the option of completely powering off the computer (such as when you are finished for the day) or of restarting the iMac (such as when you installed a new application, updated a System extension, or ran Norton Utilities to fix your hard disk).

Figure 5.5 shows the alert box that appears when you press the **Power** button. Note that you can also put your iMac to sleep (meaning that it turns itself off without losing anything that might be in volatile memory, or RAM).

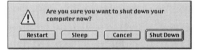

FIGURE 5.5   The Shut Down alert box.

11th Commandment   Always shut down if you can. If the iMac freezes, there is a way to sometimes shut down the application you are working in so that you can properly shut down the iMac. Press the keyboard combination ⌘+Option+Esc to "force quit." If it works, depending on the nature of the bug or freeze, this causes the Finder to override the application and quit. You lose everything that you haven't saved whenever you perform this function, so be careful and save often.

OPTIONS FOR SHUTTING DOWN

Of course, being a Mac, the iMac offers several other ways to shut down:

- Choose the Special menu and select **Shut Down** or **Restart**.

- In an emergency (a bomb or a freeze up), press the keyboard combination ⌘+Control+Power. Your iMac will restart, destroying any information that you have not saved and possibly messing up your hard drive. Do this only if you cannot shut down any other way, because this violates the 11th Commandment.

OPTIONS FOR STARTING UP

Of course, because this is a Macintosh, you are given lots of options as to which programs start up when you first turn on your iMac, as well as which programs shut down first or last when you turn off your iMac. The System Folder contains a folder for startup and shutdown items. Any type of file, alias, document, sound, or application can be placed in either of these folders and will be launched by the system at startup or shutdown. If you use an application, such as a calendar or word processor, you might want to place it, or an alias to it, in your Startup Items folder. Placing an item in the Startup Items folder will automatically open that item when you start up your iMac. Similarly, if you place an alias, file, or application on the Shut Down Items folder, the system will attempt to quit out of that software when **Shut Down** is selected from the **Special** menu, or when your iMac is set up to shut down at a particular time.

EJECTING AND THROWING THINGS AWAY

The Trash Can serves not only as a place to put items that you want to delete, but it also works as a quick way to throw away a disk or volume you no longer want on your desktop. Keep the two uses of the Trash Can separate, and you should have no problem. If you can't keep the two separate, you can use the item's contextual menu to distinguish Trash from Eject.

EJECTING DISKS AND VOLUMES

Removing CDs, removable disks, or floppies from their drives is simply a matter of throwing the icon for the drive into the Trash Can. This seems scary, but the iMac knows the difference between a drive or volume and a file or folder. As with all things Macintosh, there are other ways to remove items from your desktop:

- Select Eject from the Special menu

- Press the keyboard combination ⌘+E.

- Select the Put Away command in the File menu ⌘+Y. You can also use the contextual menu and select Put Away by pressing the Control key while clicking the item.

- Select the Move to the Trash command from the File menu ⌘+Delete.

THROWING AWAY ITEMS

The Trash Can also works to delete items from your desktop directory. Placing an item in the trash does not automatically erase it from your hard drive. You must select Empty Trash from the Special menu to formally erase the item. If you throw something away that you didn't mean to, double-click the Trash Can icon and you'll find it there (provided you haven't emptied the trash yet). Drag it out of the trash to restore it.

Maybe You Can Get It Back   Macs are very forgiving computers. If you've deleted something you really didn't mean to, and already emptied the trash, don't despair. TechTools 2.0 or Norton Utilities both have unerase features that help you retrieve deleted files most of the time (if the computer hasn't written over the file with a file with the same name).

USING COPY, CUT, PASTE, AND DRAG

Text, images, and other data can be transferred between applications and documents by using the Finder's Copy and Paste features, found in the Edit menu. Keyboard shortcuts for Copy and Paste are ⌘+C and ⌘+V, respectively. When you use the Copy function, it places any selected text, image, or other data into the iMac's Clipboard. From there, the data can be pasted into any other application or document.

Some applications also support drag-and-drop. This is even simpler than Copy and Paste, enabling you to drag an object (text, image, and so on) directly to another document or application.

If you want to select several or all the items in a window or document, you can ⬆Shift+click or ⌘+click to select specific items in the Finder or in a document. To select all items in a document or window, press ⌘+A or choose Select All from the Edit menu.

In this chapter, you learned how to get around the iMac. You learned how to use the iMac desktop, windows, and menus, how to manipulate files and folders, how to start up and shut down your iMac, how to eject and throw things away, and how to cut, copy, paste, and drag items.

Lesson 6

Getting Organized

In this lesson you will learn how to organize your desktop using aliases, the Trash Can, and the Launcher. You will also learn how to find, group, and navigate your files.

The Finder is the file manager for the Macintosh OS. Without it, you would not be able to open, close, save, print, or find files on your iMac. The most current version of Finder is called Finder 8.5.

Organizing the Desktop

Think of the desktop on the iMac as the home page of the Macintosh. Internet metaphors aside, the desktop is the starting point for iMac. It consists of Finder's menu bar, the Trash Can icon, an icon representing each hard drive and other disk volumes, and the preinstalled iMac alias files. You can rearrange these items to create a working environment best suited to your tastes and needs.

The basic tasks for organizing files and folders in iMac are simple. They involve setting up all the files and folders so that the software is easy to find and efficient to use, yet personal enough to reflect how you use your Macintosh. Organizing the desktop also involves organizing any hard drives, other types of drives, and any network servers attached to a Macintosh.

Using Aliases

The key to organizing your desktop is using the *alias*. Aliases are icons that look like the real thing (only with italicized names) but really only point to a file that is stored elsewhere on your iMac (sort of like a hypertext link on the Web). The alias of a file contains a pointer to its originating file (called, subtly enough, its *original item*).

The beauty of aliases is that they are very small files and you can put them almost anywhere on your desktop or folders. In addition, if you move or rename the original item, the alias is able to resolve the change and locate its originator. This makes it easy to move around files to make various customized organizational motifs without actually touching their actual storage location.

CREATING AN ALIAS

Creating an alias is easy. Select the file or folder you want to make an alias for and press the keyboard combination ⌘+M. You can also choose Make Alias from the File menu. Then, drag the alias to the desktop or to wherever you want it to reside. Remember that after creating an alias, you can move it, rename it, copy it, or drag and drop it as you would any file on your iMac.

Remember that after creating an alias, you can move it, rename it, copy it, or drag and drop it as you would any file on your iMac.

> **Naming an Alias**   If you decide to name the alias with exactly the same name as its original item, the two cannot reside in the same folder. If you do want to store an alias in the same location as its original item, create a subtle difference in the name, such as adding a space after the name. The alias will always appear in italics, so you will always be able to tell which is which.

You can always find the original item for an alias by selecting the alias and choosing Show Original from the File menu or the contextual menu.

MANIPULATING ALIASES

Here are some tricks to do with aliases:

- Save on confusion between throwing away things using your Trash Can and throwing away volumes or CDs using the Trash Can by creating an alias of the Trash Can, renaming it Remove Disk, and giving it a different icon.

- Place an alias of your favorite folder on the desktop. Then, whenever you want to open a favorite file, you go to the desktop level of the Open dialog box, and there is your Favorites folder in plain view. A good example of this is how Apple places an alias of a sharable folder on your desktop for your use during file sharing to restrict access to your hard disk.

- Keep track of items on removable disks by creating an alias for these files and placing the alias on your hard disk. Then, whenever you double-click the alias, the Finder asks you for the appropriate removable disk, and then opens the item. (Note that although the iMac does not include a floppy disk drive, third-party vendors such as Imation are busy developing USB-based removable drives and floppy drives to compensate for this.)

- Make an alias of your Recent Servers folder (from the Apple Menu Items folder) and put it on your desktop. Then, whenever you want to save items to an unloaded volume, select its name in your Save dialog box as the target folder.

- Avoid the Chooser to gain access to shared items by making an alias of the networked item after you have loaded it using the Chooser. Then, select the shared item's alias whenever you want to link to that item over the network.

SWEEPING CLUTTER UNDER THE RUG

The Finder has three handy features that you'll discover yourself using over and over to clear up your desktop without closing windows:

- Tear-off Application Switcher

- Hide command

- Collapse box

Use these features to keep your working area organized.

There are three ways to jump between applications and three ways to hide windows on the iMac (didn't I say that the iMac always gives you choices?). Use a combination of these tricks to move quickly around your desktop and windows. The Application menu and Application Switcher are discussed in more detail in Chapter 7 "Working With Programs." To jump quickly between applications, you can do any of the following

- Create an Application Switcher—iMac has a handy little feature for those of you who like using buttons and the Launcher to open applications. After you open your applications and documents and they are listed on the Application menu, open the Application menu and slide the mouse down its menu and off the end. Notice that the menu seems to peel off. The resulting window filled with buttons is called the *Application Switcher.* Click an application button on the Switcher to open, close, or hide windows.

- Use the Application menu—Select another application from the Application menu.

- Click another window with your mouse—If your windows are visible under the active window, click anywhere to bring that window to the front (and thereby activate it). Click the desktop to return to the Finder.

To hide open windows, you can do one of the following

- Use the Application menu's Hide command—When you want to quickly jump from the Finder to an open document, choose Hide *application name* on the Application menu to remove an application and its document from your screen and display the desktop. Alternatively, choose Hide Finder to jump back to your application while hiding any other open folders that might cause a distraction to your work.

- Set up the General Controls control panel—This hides all windows except the active one whenever you switch between applications.

- Use the Collapse button on the window you want to hide—The *WindowShade* option from System 7 is now part of every window in iMac; it's the Collapse box in the upper-right corner of each window. You can use the WindowShade option to have one or several windows open on the desktop, but with each window collapsed down to the title bar. If a window is collapsed, you can still use it to navigate through at least part of your hard drive. ⌘+click the window's name in the title bar, and a menu appears showing the path of folders in which the window resides.

> Tip   Collapse all Finder windows by holding down
> the Option key while clicking the Collapse box.

USING THE LAUNCHER

A "controversial" method for accessing applications and folders without
having to open windows is to use the Launcher Desk Accessory control
panel. I say *controversial* only because so-called power users don't use
the Launcher because it limits their capability to flexibly open and close
items. The Launcher is a venerable part of the Mac Performa line that has
been brought to iMac. I love the Launcher because I have children and do
not want them clicking away at windows. I place applications, such as
games, in the Launcher Items folder in my System Folder (dragging an
item onto the Launcher does the same thing), and they appear as buttons
on the Launcher window (see Figure 6.1).

You can set up your Launcher, as shown in Figure 6.1, with various folders, organizing your documents and files for quick startup.

To add a folder to the Launcher, do the following

1. Create a new folder with the File | New Folder command ⌘+N.

2. Rename the folder, placing a bullet in front of its name.

3. ⌘+Option-drag the new folder onto the Launcher's tab bar.

FIGURE 6.1   The Launcher provides a safe way to start applications.

Remove an item from the Launcher by pressing Option while dragging it
to the Trash Can.

VIEWING AND NAVIGATING YOUR FILES

One of the nice features of the Finder is its flexible viewing options. You can change how you view your documents and folders with a click of the mouse. Use the Views command to set up the view preference for each of your folders. Each window can be viewed differently—whether as icons or a list—based on your working style and needs.

Use Icon view if you are a visual-type person and identify things better via pictures. If you are a more analytical type and like lots of information about your files, keep your folders in List view to present a hierarchical display. A third option, for beginning users or as a safeguard for your files, is the Button view, where no one can move any items on your desktop. Figure 6.2 shows you the three different views.

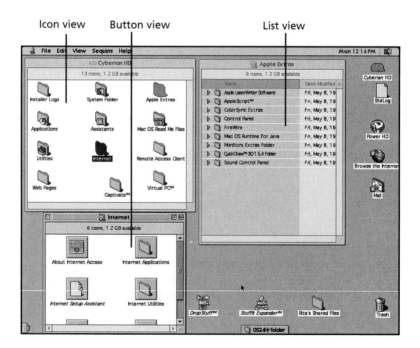

FIGURE 6.2   The List, Button, and Icon views.

Pointing and Selecting on iMac OS   There are several types of cursors in iMac. In addition to the **Magnifying Glass** icon, there is also a submenu cursor for context menus, and a plus cursor for navigating while **Option+copying** a file in Finder 8.0.

BURROWING WITH THE MOUSE

A new way to navigate through hard disks and folders, starting from your desktop, is to use your mouse. No, I don't mean double-click a folder as in System 7. Instead, hold down the mouse button at the second click instead of a double-click. When you move the mouse over a folder and keep it there for a few seconds, its icon turns into a magnifying glass and the folder automatically opens (see Figure 6.3). Apple calls this action a *click-and-a-half.*

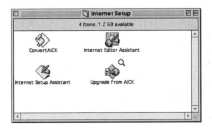

FIGURE 6.3   The **Magnifying Glass** icon provides a new navigation feature in iMac.

You can open as many folders in a row as you want. If you want to go through a different set of folders, you can move the mouse away from the current set of folders and windows, wait until they close, and then begin another navigation adventure—holding down the second click until your navigation is complete. This new way of navigating, indicated by the **Magnifying Glass** icon, enables you to quickly navigate through multiple drives, CDs, disks, and servers.

NAVIGATING WITH THE APPLE MENU AND DESKTOP

The desktop is a great place to put frequently accessed folders, files, and aliases. Another way to access folders or files quickly is to place them on the Apple menu.

- To place a folder, file, or alias on the desktop, select the file or folder icon and drag it to the desktop. Keep in mind that the file still exists on the hard drive on which it was created. Placing folders or files *on* the desktop is similar to placing them in another folder: the Desktop folder. The Desktop folder, or the desktop, is unique from other folders because it is not device-dependent. You can place files from different hard drives on the desktop, for example, without having to copy them from one drive to another.

- To place an item on the Apple menu, open the Apple Menu Items folder in the System Folder and drag an alias of the file or folder into the folder. Make it easier on yourself, and make an alias of the Apple Menu Items folder and place it inside the Apple Menu Items folder. This way, you have a way to open Apple Menu Items quickly via the Apple menu. (Are you confused yet?)

- A new Mac OS 8.5 feature is the Favorites folder. Programs that support the new Navigation Services, such as the Finder, let you add your popular files and folders to a Favorites folder by clicking the Favorites button on the Finder's Open dialog box. You can also add favorites to the Favorites folder by selecting the item—your hard disk, for example—and choosing Add to Favorites from the File menu on the desktop. The Favorites folder can be accessed from the Apple menu and from the Finder's Open dialog box (see Figure 6.4). Select the item from the Favorites submenu to open that item. You can remove items from Favorites in two ways: by using the Remove Favorites command on the Open dialog box, or by dragging unwanted favorites to the Trash Can from the Favorites folder in the System Folder.

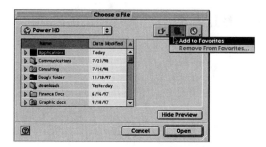

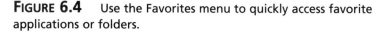

FIGURE 6.4   Use the Favorites menu to quickly access favorite applications or folders.

VIEWING DISKS, VOLUMES, AND DRIVES

The Hard Drive icon is the most frequently accessed device icon on the Macintosh, especially if you have only one drive with one partition configured on your Macintosh. Other devices that can be used with iMac include removable drives, such as Zip and Jaz 2 drives, and CD-ROMs. In addition to using the Magnifying Glass icon, a menu, or the mouse to open and close folders and files, you can select devices and their contents a number of different ways. The following list explains different ways you can select and work with files and folders stored on hard drives, CD-ROMs, and removable media.

- You can use the Tab key to select an item in a window in List, Icon, or Button view.

- You can use the arrow keys to select an item in a window in List, Icon, or Button view.

- For faster access to an item in a window, type the filename and Finder selects the filename that most closely matches what you entered.

- To rename an item, press the Return key. You can also rename a file or folder by selecting its icon and waiting a second for the name area to highlight.

- You can remove a hard drive or storage device from the desktop by placing its icon in the Trash Can, or by choosing Put Away from the File menu. *Do not throw away your Startup disk* (the one at the top-right corner of your desktop)!

FINDING FILES

Mac OS 8.5 has substantially updated the Find command (in fact it was renamed *Sherlock* to indicate its radical upgrade to something that can find anything anywhere) to include the capability to save search criteria for future searches as well as the capability to index your disk drives for rapid searching. You can search across networks and save the results via the contextual menu to the Clipboard.

There are three types of searches you can now perform in the Sherlock application:

- Sherlock a File

- Find by Content

- Search the Internet

FIND A FILE

Say you want to find a file with Mac OS in the name. Simply do the following:

1. Choose Find from the File menu (or press ⌘+F).

2. In the resulting Find dialog box, type the words **Mac OS** in the text box.

3. Click Find.

Figure 6.5 shows you the results. In this case, 199 files were found containing Mac OS. Select a file to see exactly where on your local volumes it is located. Double-click the file's name in the lower list box to open that folder.

As shown in Figure 6.6, you can select where Sherlock should seek your text by using the Name pop-up menu to change your search criteria. Use the next pop-up menu to change how precise the search should be. Click More Choices to add more search criteria and precision levels to your search.

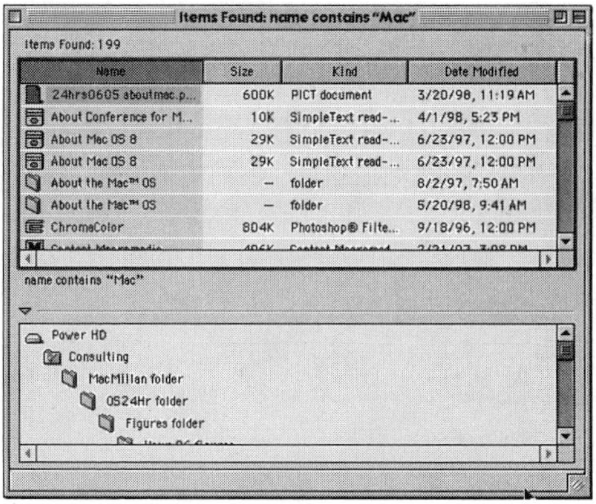

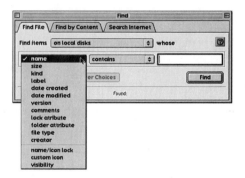

FIGURE 6.5   The Find File screen locates files based on criteria
you enter.

FIGURE 6.6   Select your search criteria and precision from the
pop-up menus.

SEARCH BY CONTENT

Here is where the neat stuff added in iMac comes into play. Say you want
to find a document containing the words Mac OS inside the document
itself, not just within the filename or Finder headings. You can perform a
search of your local and networked disks using the content search engine.

1. Open Find or select Sherlock from the Apple menu.

2. Click the Search Content tab. Figure 6.7 shows you the resulting
   Find window.

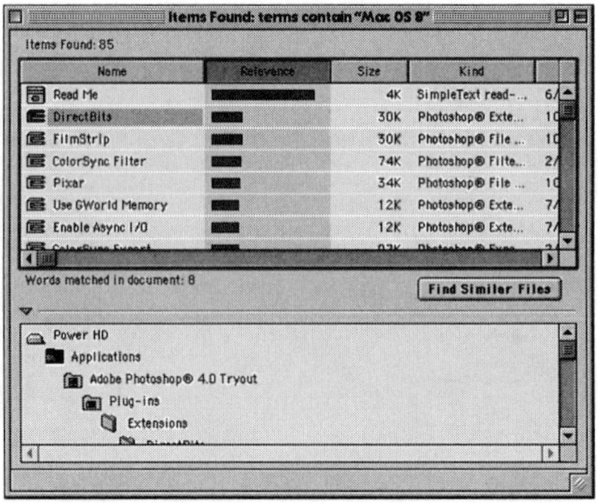

FIGURE 6.7   Files containing your search phrase are listed in the dialog box.

3. Select a volume to search and type the text you want to find in the Text box. In this case, I chose iMac.

4. The search might take some time based on how large your disk drives are and how many you chose to search.

You can speed up the search time by indexing your drives. Indexing creates a mini-database of all the major words in all your documents on your selected drive. (Note that little words, such as the, and, a, and so forth are deleted to shorten the list). Find uses this index to speed up its search. To index your drives, do the following:

1. Click the Index button on the bottom of the Search by Content screen.

2. In the resulting dialog box (shown in Figure 6.8), select a disk drive and click Index.

3. You can schedule updates to the Index at regular intervals to ensure that the Index is up-to-date.

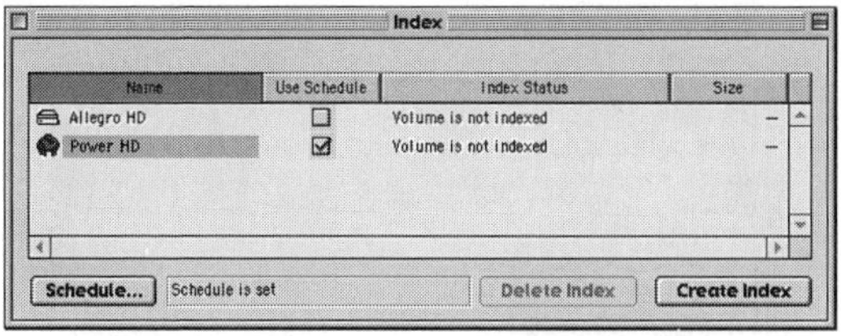

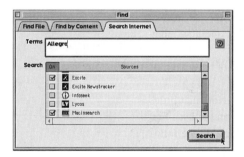

FIGURE 6.8   Indexing your volumes speeds up the search time.

SEARCH THE INTERNET

Here is a really cool new feature of Sherlock: Now you can search the Internet for any phrase you type into the Find dialog box. You can also select where on the Internet you want to search. Narrow or broaden your search by selecting different search engines and Web sites, such as Excite or Yahoo!. Figure 6.9 shows you a search I performed for the word Allegro. When I clicked Find, Remote Access dialed my ISP and initiated the search.

FIGURE 6.9   Search the Internet for any topic by typing a phrase in the Search Internet window.

The results of my search are displayed in Figure 6.10. Clicking a link automatically opens my browser to that page. You can add search engines and your favorite encyclopedia sites to the list of searchable sites.

Sherlock lets you save all the search criteria you created in each of the three types of searches. Select Save Search Criteria from the File menu in the Find application. If you want to use these criteria, select Open Search Criteria from the File menu of the Sherlock application.

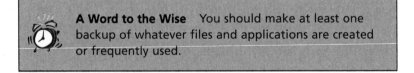

Items Found: terms contain "allegro"

Items Found: 9

Name	Relevance	Site
The upcoming OS update	—	www.macinsearch.com
Apple rethinks OS schedules refines featu...	—	www.macinsearch.com
NewTech: the Mac technology column	—	www.macinsearch.com
Mac OS Rumors	—	www.macinsearch.com
TidBITS#53/08-Apr-91	—	www.macinsearch.com
Macs, Mac Clones & Rhapsody	—	www.macinsearch.com
Mac Manager: Mac OS has legs all right	—	www.macinsearch.com

terms contain "allegro"

[1/#07 - The upcoming OS update
[NEWS] 4/24/98 Mac OS 8.2 to gain PPC code, new look Clifford Colby Apple is
reportedly working on an overhaul of the Mac OS that will combine a face lift with major
revisions beneath the surface. Sources said the project, code-named Allegro, is expected to
be ...

FIGURE 6.10   Click a link to open that page in your browser.

OPENING AND GROUPING DOCUMENTS

Another regular regimen on your computer is opening and saving documents. To make it easier to find files to open, try grouping related files in
the same folder. You can group files and folders in several different ways.
The most common method is to use a unique filename so that you can tell
what the document is about, or who it is from or for. You can also customize file and folder groupings by adding a space at the beginning of the
name of a file or folder, or by assigning a common label across selected
items. To assign a label to any file or folder, select the item, and then
choose a label color from the **Label** pull-down menu located in the **File**
menu or contextual menu. The selected file or folder displays the selected
label color.

> **A Word to the Wise**   You should make at least one
> backup of whatever files and applications are created
> or frequently used.

DRAGGING VERSUS DOUBLE-CLICKING FILES

Double-clicking a file is probably the most intuitive way to open a file
and its application. You can also choose **Open** from the **File** or contextual
menu or press ⌘+O to open files. Another way to open a file is to drag its

icon over the icon of the application with which you want to open the file. Some applications also support dragging the file into an already open window to open the file.

Dragging a file over the application you want to use can save more time than double-clicking the file. For example, if you have more than one application on your hard disk that can read text files, double-clicking a file might not open the application you want to use. Also, if Easy Open is enabled, it will show a list of applications that might be capable of opening the file.

USING THE TRASH CAN

The Trash Can is, as its name denotes, a place to remove files and folders from iMac (see Figure 6.11). The Trash Can icon appears to be empty when no files are in the Trash Can; a full Trash Can icon appears when the Trash Can contains files or folders. The Trash Can icon is similar to the hard drive device icon; you cannot place it into another window or remove it from the desktop. The Trash Can is also similar to the desktop in the sense that when you share files, the Trash Can is a folder.

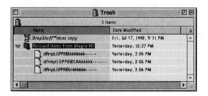

FIGURE 6.11   You can view items in the trash in List mode.

EMPTYING THE TRASH CAN

There are no serious penalties for waiting to take out the trash. You can place items in the Trash Can until you are sure you want to delete them. Double-clicking the Trash Can icon opens a window in which you can view items in List, Button, or Icon mode. To remove items from the Trash Can, choose Empty Trash from the Special menu. A warning message asks you to confirm whether you want to remove the items permanently. If you put a file or folder from a server into the Trash Can, the trash will be emptied when the server is dismounted from the desktop. Select

Cancel if you want to keep an item in the trash. To bypass the warning message, hold down the Option key while selecting Empty Trash from the Special menu.

> **You Don't Have to be Warned**   The warning for emptying the Trash Can be turned off from the Get Info pull-down menu. The General Information window for the Trash Can icon contains a Warn Before Emptying check box at the bottom of its window; uncheck this check box to turn the warning off.

Most files and folders are deleted when you empty the trash. Some files, however, can be locked or busy, resulting in a dialog box telling you those types of files could not be deleted. For locked files, hold down the Option key while selecting Empty Trash. If a file is busy, try restarting the computer to make the file "un-busy," and then select Empty Trash.

After files or folders are deleted, they are removed from Finder's access. However, they are still on the hard drive. As new files or folders are created, they will most likely be created over the hard disk where the previous deleted file was physically located on the disk. If you accidentally delete a file, you can use software such as Norton Utilities to recover it. Remember not to create or copy any additional files or folders onto the drive until after the file or folder you need has been recovered.

Occasionally, when iMac crashes or freezes, a folder titled Rescued items from *hard drive name* appears in the Trash Can. iMac uses the folder and its items to help restart system software. After you successfully restart the computer, you can delete the folder and its items without harming the iMac.

THE MOVE TO TRASH COMMAND

A new feature in iMac is the *Move to Trash command* in any file or folder's context menu. Selecting Move to Trash for any item places that item directly in the trash. You can also select an item, and then press ⌘+delete to move files or folders to the Trash Can.

USING THE GENERAL INFORMATION WINDOW

The General Information dialog box contains many different types of information about an application, such as

- When it was created

- Where it is located on the disk

- How much memory it needs to run

To see the General Information window, select an application icon, such as SimpleText, and select General Information from the Get Info pull-down menu on the File menu. The following list identifies each item in the General Information window of an application:

- The Suggested Size is the amount of memory recommended to run the application. You cannot modify this number.

- The Minimum Size is the amount of memory the application must have to launch. For example, SimpleText has a Preferred Size of 512KB, and a Minimum Size of 192KB. Even if 512KB is not available in Finder, for example, SimpleText can open as long as there is more than 192KB of available memory. This number can be adjusted to be higher or lower than the Suggested Size.

- The Preferred Size is the amount of memory the application will use when opened. For many applications, you can increase this number, especially if working with large files. The recommended size varies from 20 percent up to a ratio based on the size of the file you want to open with the application.

> **Use Virtual Memory to Decrease Memory Requirements**   In Mac OS 8.1 and higher, the default configuration has added 1MB of virtual memory to decrease the amount of RAM an application uses.

The General Information window is the key to setting how much memory an application uses when it is open. If the preferred amount of memory is not available, the application will run in any amount of memory available between the minimum and preferred settings. For Power Macintosh computers, the note at the bottom of the window informs you of how much memory you can save if virtual memory is enabled.

This lesson showed you how to organize your desktop by using aliases, the Trash Can, and the Launcher. You also learned how to find, view, group, and navigate your files.

Lesson 7

Working with Programs

In this lesson you will learn how to work with programs, including installing, opening, closing, removing, and saving applications. You will also learn how to multitask on the iMac.

The term *application* refers to the file that you double-click and run on a Mac. It also refers to the user interface, functions, and all the software that might be required to make it work, such as data files, shared libraries, preferences, images, databases, or networking software. The iMac lets you work with more than one application at a time. *Background processing* allows you to copy files, throw away trash, or print while you are working in an application. One of the biggest advantages of Finder 8.5 is its new capability to multitask in this manner.

Installing and Removing Applications

Installers are designed to simplify application installation and to compress installed files in order to reduce the floppy disk or media footprint for the product; some installers also support removing the software.

Installing Applications

In general, most software installers put all installed pieces into one folder on the hard drive. Some installers also put preference settings and support files in the System Folder. Some also have control panels or extensions placed in the System Folder, but these can be identified by using Extensions Manager control panel.

In any case, you can begin installing the software in question by inserting the media (CD-ROM) into your drive and following the instructions that appear as part of the installation program.

REMOVING APPLICATIONS

The easiest way to remove applications is to first check the original installer to see whether there is a Remove option. If not, drag the main software folder for that application to the Trash Can. Then use Sherlock to look for related files, and trash those as well. Be sure that any support files you find aren't used by other applications before you trash them (for example, many Microsoft applications share support files).

Application Protection   iMac creates an Application folder at the root level of the hard drive if one does not already exist. To protect the software in that folder, there is a Protect an Application setting in the General Controls control panel. If this setting is active, the system will not let you move any files or folders out of the Application folder. If you need to remove or reorganize software in this folder, turn off this setting, uncheck the Protect Applications folder check box in the General Controls control panel, and then you can make changes.

OPENING, CLOSING, AND SAVING DOCUMENTS

Mac OS 8.5 introduces a new Finder dialog box called Navigation Services that lets you rapidly find and open or save files on your local hard drive or across networks. In addition, you can select from previously opened documents using a new pull-down menu called Favorites. You will only see these new Finder dialogs where software has been updated to support its services until software vendors upgrade their programs to take advantage of the enhanced searching capabilities of Navigation Services.

In most applications you will continue to see the older Finder dialog boxes displayed in Figure 7.1. This Open dialog box from Word 98 has been enhanced by Microsoft to enable you to find a file using Microsoft's Find File function from within the dialog box.

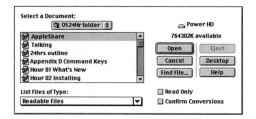

FIGURE 7.1 Word 98 still uses the older Finder Open dialog box.

OPENING APPLICATIONS

As with all things Macintosh, there are various ways to open an application and its documents:

- Select the application or document icon you want to open. Choose Open from the File menu.

- Select the application or document you want to open and press the keyboard combination ⌘+O.

- Double-click the document you want to open, or if you aren't currently working on a document, double-click the application's icon.

- Place an alias of the application or document in the Launcher, and then click its icon when you want to open it.

- Drag the document you want to open on top of the icon of its application. If you have MacLink Plus installed (it comes with iMac), you can drag a document onto any application and MacLink finds the appropriate application to open it.

The Navigation Services-based Open dialog box is extremely useful. As shown in Figure 7.2, the Finder list box is arranged so that you can navigate using the same arrow and folder metaphors you use to navigate folders and files on the desktop in List view. In addition, contextual menus work in the dialog box.

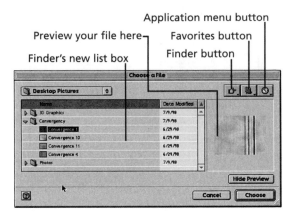

FIGURE 7.2   The new Finder Open dialog box provides ways to backtrack to previously opened items.

USING NAVIGATION SERVICES

Navigation Services has some neat features. Using the three new buttons located on the top-right of the dialog box (refer to Figure 7.2), you can open documents locally or on the Internet or network, collect files you use regularly and place them in a Favorites folder, or go to a recently accessed document with the click of your mouse.

There are three buttons on the right side of the dialog box:

- The Finder button   The "Pointing Finger" button, which I call the *Finder* button, lets you access files both locally and remotely. This button replaces the arduous routine of clicking the Desktop button, selecting a new volume, scrolling through the volume to a select folder, and so forth to switch hard drives or networks. Instead, you simply click the Finder button, and then use the pop-up menu that appears to open a new volume from those listed.

- The Favorites button   Clicking the "Book Shelf" button, which I call the *Favorites* button, opens your Favorites pop-up menu.

You can add files to Favorites by selecting a file in the Finder list box and choosing Add To Favorites. You can choose a previously selected favorite by selecting it from the menu. You can also add folders or files to the Favorites pop-up menu from the File menu on the desktop using the Add To Favorites command.

• The Application menu button   Clicking the "Clock" button, which I call the *Application menu* button, lists documents you have recently selected. Here is where Navigation Services shines, because you can get to your regularly used documents without drilling through folders by selecting from this pop-up menu. It does not matter whether the document is stored locally or remotely.

Closing Windows and Applications

Closing an application can also be performed in several ways, depending on whether you want to end your working session (quit) or just close a document to begin a new one (close).

If you want to totally end a working session, use the Quit command from the File menu or press the keyboard combination ⌘+Q. Using the Quit command gives the application the chance to save any unsaved materials prior to quitting. You get a Save dialog box after using the Quit command if you haven't saved since the last change.

Use the Close command on the File menu ⌘+W to close a window, such as a document. Another way to close a window but remain in an application is to click the Close box on the top-left side of a window.

 Close Everything   You can close all open windows by pressing the Option key while clicking a Close box or while pressing ⌘+W.

SAVING DOCUMENTS

Save early and save often.

There are several ways to save your data. If you have already given your document a name, choosing Save from the File menu will save information to your previously named file. You can also press the keyboard combination ⌘+S. Many applications have added a toolbar button for saving to make the task even easier.

If you have not previously named your document, using the Save command opens a very special Finder dialog box called Save As. Use this dialog box to assign a name to your document as well as a place where you want to save it. In the Save As dialog box, you see the Finder's standard list box and navigation buttons. Use these tools to select a folder where you want to save your document. Type a name for your document in the Text box. You can then select a file format, such as Word 98, RTF, or Word 2 (Word for Windows 95), in which you want to save your document. Select the format from the Format pop-up menu.

The Save As command has another very powerful use: renaming or relocating files. Renaming and relocating files is an excellent way to produce fast backup copies of your critical documents. You can rename files to separate your Windows versions from your Mac versions (by adding that DOS suffix to the Windows version), or separating different versions of a document by numbering the revisions in its name. You can access the Save As command at any time by choosing the File menu and selecting Save As.

> **Changes Coming**   The Save As dialog box is slated to change to a format similar to the one you saw in the new Open dialog box. Because you won't be able to use this easier Navigation Services–based box until software vendors update their applications to support the new function, I can't show you an example of the new box in this book.

DOING MORE THAN ONE TASK WITH iMAC

Multitasking with iMac can mean having two, three, or more applications open at the same time (see Figure 7.3). While these are running, you can also copy several files and folders across several windows, at the same time deleting files or folders from the trash. Multitasking lets you perform a number of different Finder tasks such as copying, deleting, or formatting media, while also accessing applications that run in the foreground or background.

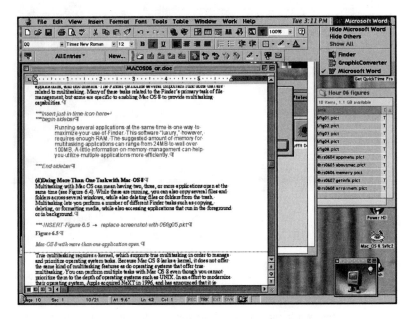

FIGURE 7.3   iMac with more than one application open.

WORKING WITH THE APPLICATION MENU

The Application menu is the visible manifestation of the iMac's multitasking functions at work. You use this menu to switch between active windows, show or hide active windows, and return to the Finder. Figure 7.4 shows the open Application menu displaying several open programs as well as an indication of the currently active application.

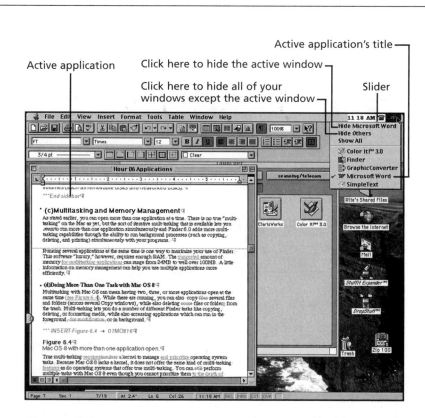

FIGURE 7.4   The Application menu lets you switch between open applications.

I keep throwing around the word *active*. The easiest way to define an *active window* is to say that it is the one on top. You can perform work in an active window's document. Active windows are indicated by a fully drawn title bar, while inactive windows are grayed out and lie behind the active window. Just to confuse you, you can switch between active and inactive windows by clicking a window lying beneath your active window to bring it to the front, thereby making it the active window.

There can be only one application active at one time; the *active application* is the one that is running in the active window. (I am not counting background processes such as copying, printing, or moving in my definition of active applications for simplicity's sake.)

Mac OS 8.5 provides several new features to enhance the power of the Application menu:

- You can switch between applications without even opening the Application menu by pressing ⌘+Tab. This Program Switcher switches you between applications in the order they appear on the Application menu.

- You can display the active application's name in your menu bar along with its icon (for those of you who can't remember what the icon for your program represents). If you don't like to use precious menu bar space with long application names, use the Slider to move the name off the bar.

- You can select the Application menu and slide the mouse down the menu and past the end. Notice that a shadow menu follows your cursor onto the desktop. This tear-off palette is called the *Application Switcher*; you can use the Switcher's buttons to switch between or close applications.

This chapter explained how to work with programs, including installing, removing, opening, closing, and saving applications. It also covered how to close windows and save documents, and how to multitask on the iMac.

LESSON 8

CUSTOMIZING THE DESKTOP

In this lesson you will learn how to customize your iMac, from setting desktop themes to selecting desktop sounds. You will also learn how to use various control panels to affect how your keyboard behaves.

Let's begin by exploring how to change the way iMac looks. You have a lot of control over how your desktop appears, including menu bars, fonts, window formats, scrollbars, coloring, and highlights. You can add *wallpaper*, including various tiled designs, to the desktop background, or you can add photographs that brighten your working atmosphere.

THE APPEARANCE CONTROL PANEL

If you are familiar with older Mac system software, you know that you can change the appearance of the desktop, including its background, how windows are drawn, and how windows behave. Mac OS 8.5 introduces a new Appearance control panel, which takes over the control of how your desktop looks, sounds, and behaves. With this control panel you can set up desktop themes consisting of a desktop picture, background colors, highlight colors, sounds, and fonts, as well as set how you want the overall window to behave. The Appearance control panel consists of six screens:

- Themes
- Appearance
- Fonts
- Desktop
- Sounds
- Options

> **Differences Between Mac OS 8.1 and Mac OS 8.5**
> One of the most extensive differences between Mac OS 8.1 that comes installed on early iMacs and Mac OS 8.5 is in the new function of the Appearance control panel. Mac OS 8.1 requires the installation of the Appearance control panel to start up properly, but most of the interesting desktop customization features appear in the Desktop Pictures control panel (namely the capability to change the look and some behavior of the desktop image). Mac OS 8.5 has removed the Appearance control panel from the system and created a new toolbox manager called the *Appearance Manager* that controls all aspects of desktop appearance including images, fonts, sounds, windowing behavior, color highlighting, and so forth. For the purposes of this book, it is assumed that you have Mac OS 8.5 installed. Try not to get confused between the Desktop Pictures and Appearance control panels; just know that Mac OS 8.5 subsumes Desktop Pictures' functions into the Appearance control panel.

SETTING DESKTOP THEMES

The quickest way to change the appearance of your desktop is to select a desktop theme from those included with the Appearance control panel. I am assuming that hackers and shareware gurus will add to this list in the future. Right now, there is only one official desktop theme to choose from, namely *Platinum*. You can create custom themes based on Platinum by changing desktop pictures, fonts, sounds, and so forth. These customized variations are also called *themes* just to confuse you.

To set up your machine to use a particular theme, do the following:

1. Open the Appearance control panel from the Control Panels pull-down menu on the Apple menu and click the Themes tab to its window.

2. Scroll through the themes and click the one you want to use.

3. Your desktop changes to accommodate your choice.

If you use the other five tabs, you are given the option of saving your customized desktop as a new theme. Always return to the Themes tab to save your new desktop.

SETTING THE DESKTOP APPEARANCE

You can change the highlighting color used by applications to select items as well as by the system to indicate the status of processes using the Appearance control panel's Appearance tab (see Figure 8.1). The Appearance tab lets you use the Color Picker to select a custom highlight color for both text and status markers. You are also given the option of changing the theme used to draw menu bars and windows.

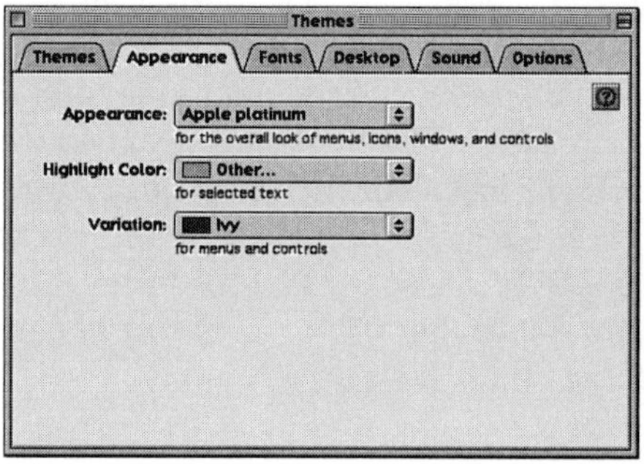

FIGURE 8.1   The Appearance tab enables you to choose highlight colors.

SETTING DESKTOP FONTS

In System 7, you could change how system text was displayed using the View Options command. Now, however, you can change the way menu bars, title bars, system text, and dialog box text are displayed in both the Finder and on the desktop using the handy Font tab on the Appearance control panel (see Figure 8.2).

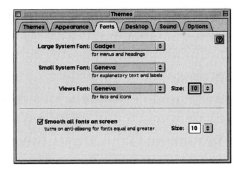

FIGURE 8.2   The Fonts tab lets you choose three types of system fonts.

Don't Overdo It   Don't go crazy with your selections, such as using Sand for Menu bars or London for File names. You'll kill your eyes.

SETTING DESKTOP PATTERNS AND PICTURES

Desktop patterns have been on Macintosh computers since System 1.0; back then it was a simple gray background. System 7.5 added a Desktop Patterns control panel to make it easier to create and share patterns with other Macintosh computers. Originally, desktop patterns were an 8×8-pixel square repeated across the desktop. With System 7.5, desktop patterns extended the desktop pattern size to range from 8×8 to 128×128. Desktop Pictures under Mac OS 8.1 support these same features and also named these bitmapped small drawings with descriptions for easier selection. In addition, Mac OS 8.1 introduced the capability to add photographic images to the desktop, called *desktop pictures*. Mac OS 8.5 updated desktop pictures by placing the functions of this and the older desktop Patterns control panel into the Appearance control panel. Simply click the Desktop tab to select either patterns or pictures.

SELECTING DESKTOP PATTERNS

You can adjust the images that appear on the desktop from solid colors to tiled bitmapped drawings and JPEG-compressed photographs. The size and amount of memory required for each pattern displays below the pattern in the control panel. All patterns work in any color depth mode, but 256 or more colors are recommended. To set a pattern, do the following:

1. Select a pattern name from the Patterns list box.

2. An example of the pattern is shown in the box to the left of the list.

3. If you like the pattern, click Set desktop to set it or double-click the pattern.

SELECTING DESKTOP PICTURES

Desktop pictures are actual JPEG-compressed photographs and are designed to fill the desktop with one picture. Any PICT file or photograph can be used as a desktop picture. These images do not need to be any particular size, but if you have a 17- or 20-inch monitor, an 832×624 image is a good size to use for a high-resolution desktop picture image. If the desktop picture you want to use is smaller than the desktop itself, the desktop pattern will fill out the rest of the desktop.

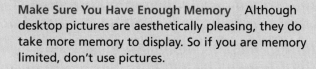

Make Sure You Have Enough Memory Although desktop pictures are aesthetically pleasing, they do take more memory to display. So if you are memory limited, don't use pictures.

To select a desktop picture, do the following:

1. Click the Place Picture button on the Appearance control panel's Desktop tab. If youalready have a desktop picture displayed, the button says Remove Picture. Click this first then click Place Picture.

2. A new Navigation Services Open dialog box shows the available photographs, with a preview to the left of the selected file. Click the file you want to use to select it.

3. Click Open.

4. The chosen file appears in the Desktop tab of the Appearance control panel (the image's dimensions and memory reqirements appear below the image). click the Set desktop button to pur the selected picture on to the desktop.

SETTING DESKTOP SOUNDS

The Appearance control panel lets you set individual sounds for different system functions, such as opening files, closing windows, throwing things away, and other activities. Click the Sound tab to display the screen shown in Figure 8.3. Select the system features you want to apply sounds to then select the sound theme you want to apply (again for now, your options are Gizmo, Hi-Tech, or Platinum).

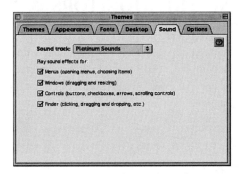

FIGURE **8.3**   The Sound tab lets you choose sounds for system functions such as opening and closing windows or selecting items.

SETTING OTHER DESKTOP OPTIONS

The final screen on the Appearance control panel provides the opportunity to change how your windows scroll. You can opt to place the scroll arrows on the top, bottom, or both ends. This screen also lets you control how your scrollbars work (whether they change shape when you resize a window getting longer and shorter or whether they function like they always have in earlier operating system versions). The Options tab (see Figure 8.4) also allows you to turn on or off the Windowshade feature (this refers to your capability to minimize or maximize windows down to their title bar).

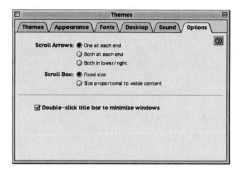

FIGURE 8.4   The Options tab lets you choose how your windows scroll as well as the appearance of scroll arrows and scrollbars.

CHANGING THE MONITORS & SOUND CONTROL PANEL

The Monitors & Sound control panel was introduced with the first PCI Power Macintosh computers in 1995, and it has been updated with some new features. Because the iMac offers a built-in monitor, the Monitors & Sound control panel has been modified to provide the capability to adjust the vertical and horizontal signals as well as the color and resolution of the display.

SIZING UP YOUR MONITOR

The Monitors & Sound control panel lets you switch resolutions and bit depths to match your working requirements. I like to work with larger icons and text, so I keep my monitor set at 800×600 pixels and thousands of colors. If you want to see more territory on your screen, set a higher resolution.

The Monitor section of the control panel consists of two areas:

- Color Depth
- Resolution

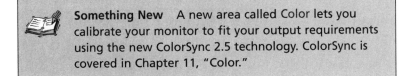

Something New   A new area called Color lets you calibrate your monitor to fit your output requirements using the new ColorSync 2.5 technology. ColorSync is covered in Chapter 11, "Color."

COLOR DEPTH

Color Depth consists of three interrelated settings:

- A list of color depths

- A radio button for grays or colors

- A color table

Depending on the color depth selected in the list, the color table changes to reflect the current system color palette. The Grays radio button only applies to Black & White, 4, 16, and 256 color depth settings. Only the Color radio button is selectable in Thousands and Millions color depth modes.

RESOLUTION

The resolution of the monitor is related to the size of the desktop. This area of the control panel consists of two settings:

- A pop-up-menu with recommended settings

- A list of supported monitor resolutions

Selecting any resolution updates the screen automatically.

CHANGING THE ALERT SOUNDS

The Simple Beep is the default alert sound for iMac, but the Monitors & Sounds control panel contains a short list of alert sounds from which you can choose. These sound files are stored in the system file. Any sound recorded in this control panel (see Figure 8.5) is also stored in the system file.

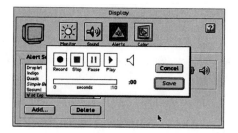

FIGURE 8.5   The Alert screen of Monitors & Sound control panel and Recording window.

The Monitors & Sound control panel's Alert window consists of three distinct functions:

- System Alert Volume

- Alert Sound list

- Alert Recording button (Add button)

You can set the System Alert Volume at any setting between zero and seven. This volume level also affects the computer system volume level.

The Add and Delete buttons at the bottom of the window enable you to create or remove any sounds from the Alert Sound list. Add brings up a simple recording window with the following controls:

- Record

- Stop

- Pause

- Play

The recording level of a connected microphone or audio CD is reflected in animation from the Speaker icon. Selecting the Save button in the Recording window adds the recorded sound to the Alert sound list.

> **Record Your Own Sounds**   To record alert sounds for iMac, you can also select Simple Sound in the Apple menu, or the Sound control panel in the Apple Extras folder.

CHANGING THE KEYBOARD CONTROL PANEL

The Keyboard control panel affects all iMac OS systems despite the fact that the top half of the control panel is specific to international keyboard layouts.

You can select any number of keyboard layouts to support the appropriate keyboard for that country or language. Changing the keyboard layout in the Keyboard menu changes the keyboard layout used by iMac. For example, if you check the French or German keyboard layout in the Keyboard control panel, a Flag icon appears in the Keyboard menu bar after you close the Keyboard control panel. Select French or German from this menu, and then open the KeyCaps desk accessory from the Apple menu to see how the keyboard layout has changed. You can rotate between keyboard layouts by choosing the Command-Option-Space bar check box in this control panel.

> **Where's the Keyboard Menu?**   If only one keyboard layout is selected in the Keyboard control panel, the Keyboard menu does not appear in the menu bar.

Settings for keyboard repeat behaviors are located at the bottom of the Keyboard control panel. These settings affect almost all keys on the keyboard, except for the Command, Option, Control, Caps Lock, and Escape keys. Pressing any key on the keyboard causes a Macintosh computer to type that key repeatedly as long as the key is held down.

This can affect you if you use any alphabet keys for playing games or for inputting repetitive characters with your computer. Key Repeat options include slow to fast key repeat rates, and short to long (or off) settings for the Delay Until Repeat option.

MODIFYING THE NUMBERS CONTROL PANEL

The Numbers control panel can work with keyboard layout scripts in the Keyboard control panel, or it can have its own settings, independent of other language settings in iMac. The Numbers control panel enables you to select how numbers are displayed in Finder and applications. The number formats available in the Numbers control panel are resources installed in the System file. Choosing the number format, Decimal, and Thousands options is easier in iMac with sticky menus and the pop-up menu in the Numbers control panel.

Use the Number Format field to select from Australian, Brasil, British, Danish, Dutch, Finnish, Flemish, French, French Canadian, German, Italian, Norwegian, Spanish, Swedish, Swiss French, Swiss German, Swiss Italian, or U.S. The number format can be the same or completely different from the keyboard layout selected in the Keyboard control panel. You can set the number format to match the settings in the Keyboard control panel, and also check the Text control panel to make certain that the text behavior for the keyboard layout also matches the number format.

MODIFYING THE TEXT CONTROL PANEL

The Text control panel (see Figure 8.6) works with or independently of the Keyboard and Numbers control panels. It displays text behaviors for script resources installed in the System file. All keyboard layouts installed with iMac use Roman script resources installed in the System file. Language kits for two-byte languages, however, such as Chinese, Japanese, and Korean, or complex one-byte languages add more items to the pop-up menu in the Text control panel.

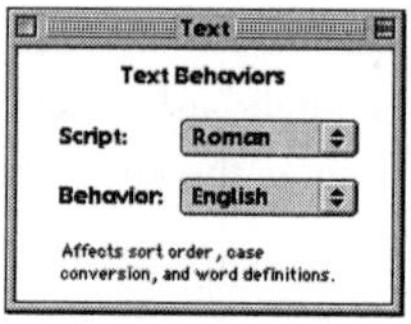

FIGURE 8.6   The Text control panel.

Both pop-up menus have the new grayscale look for iMac. Sticky menus enable you to click the Behavior menu, and thereby display all items. The default settings for iMac in the United States are Roman script with English behavior. To change the text behavior, select from Brasil, Danish, Dutch, English, Finnish, French, French Canadian, German, Italian, Norwegian, Spanish, and Swedish. Changes made to this control panel are independent of sort order, case conversion, and word definitions in Finder and any applications.

MORE CUSTOMIZATION OPTIONS

Of course, there are even more ways to change the look, feel, and function of iMac. The Appearance, Extensions Manager, File Sharing, Keyboard, Numbers, Text, and Monitors & Sound control panels are provided with iMac to customize a wide range of Finder features. A wider range of shareware and commercial software provides additional ways of modifying Finder features.

Caution   Your iMac can become unstable as a result of combining extensions and control panels in the System Folder. Some software that modifies the way Finder looks or works might have software conflicts with existing system software or other software installed with your computer.

This lesson covers how to customize your iMac, from setting desktop themes to selecting desktop sounds. It also shows you how to adjust your monitor for best results. Finally, you learned how to use various control panels to affect how your keyboard and other features behave.

LESSON 9

FONTS

In this lesson you will learn about the WSIWYG technology. You will also learn about how to share fonts between computers, how to install fonts, how to view fonts, and how to add professional touches to your documents.

The goal in a WYSIWYG (pronounced "wizzy wig" and short for "What You See Is What You Get") environment is to have what appears onscreen to be as close as possible to what appears on the printed page. Text and graphics can be intermixed intuitively, both onscreen and on paper. Graphics are drawn on the screen directly—without having to go into other modes of operation—and text is displayed as it will print. Although it is not an inherent requirement of a WYSIWYG environment, flexibility in the type and style of characters used for text has played an important role in its popularity.

This flexibility in character styles, along with the capability to mix text and graphics, has revolutionized how personal computers are used. Macintosh introduced the concept of publishing on the desktop to the business world. The horizons have expanded even further with the concepts of color desktop publishing, desktop animation, desktop sound studios, and desktop multimedia.

SHARING FONTS BETWEEN COMPUTERS

Much care has been taken to ensure that fonts print correctly, but not as much care has been taken to ensure that fonts display correctly or can be transported easily between computer systems. This portability issue is the new frontier of font development.

Because there is such a problem when you want to read a document created on one computer on another, software vendors such as Adobe, Microsoft, and Apple have been working diligently on ways to transport font information between computers and platforms. One of the developments that allow computers to display documents accurately and printers to print documents accurately—even if the proper fonts are not resident— is a new Type 1 font called *Multiple Master Fonts*. All these font formats are converging into a single open system called *OpenType*. Adobe and Microsoft developed OpenType to absorb TrueType and PostScript font technologies into a single package that holds information for both outline and bitmapped font images. Mac OS 8.5 supports OpenType.

INSTALLING FONTS

System 7.1 introduced an innovation called the Font folder to clean up the System Folder. Mac OS 8 carries on this tradition but adds to its convenience. Screen fonts are kept in *font suitcases* containing combinations of TrueType and bitmapped fonts. You can open a suitcase by double-clicking it to reveal its contents.

Using the Font Folder   The one side effect of using the Font folder is that any font placed into the folder is "on" or loaded into memory during your iMacís startup, thus using precious memory even if you do not want to use that font during your present work or play.

Applications that install fonts, such as Microsoft Word 98 or CorelDraw 8, will place these fonts in the Font folder. If you are using a font manager, you can drag the fonts out of the Font folder after their installation and use a font manager, such as ATM Deluxe, to also manage these fonts. Periodically review the contents of your Font folder for new inclusions.

To place fonts in the Font folder, drag the font from the Fonts window on to the System Folder. Be sure to quit all programs before installing fonts, because open programs will not register the installation.

FONT FAMILIES AND WYSIWYG FONTS

Computer fonts are based on a very old technology (remember Gutenburg and his printed Bible in the fourteenth century?). Type is generally spoken of as families that include all of the styles (plain, bold, italic, and bold italic).

PostScript fonts actually provide four printer files (or more for condensed, extended, light, black, or other cousins). Any PostScript font installed on your iMac is automatically displayed in the application Font menus without any organization other than alphabetical, making for very long and cryptic lists of fonts. In fact, a lot of fonts are listed by their font foundry IDs, making for even more confusion. Luckily, you can install a font family manager such as Adobe Type Reunion 2.0 (see Figure 9.1). Type Reunion is one of several WYSIWYG Font Menu managers (Font Juggler is another) that arrange fonts into their constituent families and display the resulting font family name just as it appears onscreen. Type Reunion and Font Juggler also further organize your fonts into sets for each project you undertake.

FIGURE 9.1   Adobe Type Reunion displays your fonts by family in their actual forms so you don't have to grope for the perfect font.

VIEWING FONTS

You can see a sample of your font by double-clicking its icon. If the font is a TrueType font, it displays representative text in three sizes: 9, 12, and 18 points (see Figure 9.2). If the font is a bitmap or PostScript font, it displays representative text only for the font size you selected (see Figure 9.3).

FIGURE 9.2 The TrueType window displays text representing three sizes of Helvetica.

FIGURE 9.3 The Screen font window displays text representing 12-point Helvetica.

ADDING PROFESSIONAL POLISH

The goal of all layout is to increase the readability of a document. The spaces between words and lines, as well as the size and proportions of the type used in a document, are very important tools for this purpose.

The Macintosh's WYSIWYG display enables you to enhance your documents by adding different typefaces, styles, and sizes. Because you control what your document will look like, you must become a layout artist to use the Macintosh to its fullest potential. Over the years, commercial artists and layout specialists have developed rules-of-thumb to assist them in creating documents that are easy to read and yet strongly convey the information they were meant to convey.

> **Don't Overdo It**   The first rule in using fonts wisely is to not use a lot of different fonts on a page. Use at most two fonts—a heading font and a text font. You can vary the heading levels by changing the typeface of the heading font, but use the same font for all headings.

SERIF VERSUS SANS SERIF

All fonts fall into two categories:

- Serif
- Sans serif

Studies have shown that serif fonts are more readable in extended text than sans-serif fonts. The thick and thin variations in serif fonts enable the eye to move naturally across a page without getting lost in the similarity of the shapes (see Figure 9.4).

> **Tip**   When using both a sans-serif font and a serif font on a single page, use contrasting typefaces to increase the impact. For instance, if the serifs font is light and airy, use a strong bold sans-serif font for the headings.

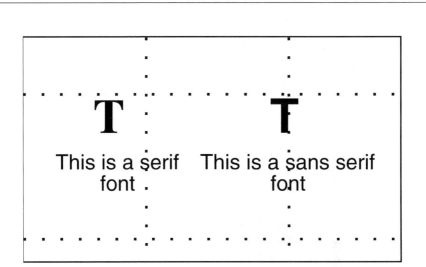

FIGURE 9.4   Serif and sans-serif fonts serve different purposes in a document.

KERNING

Kerning is a technical term for removing small spaces between letters to create visually consistent spacing. You kern letters to create the optical illusion that they appear more consistently evenly spaced on the page. The key to correct application of kerning is your visual perception of words versus the white space between words. Each character in proportional type creates its own perception of size and shape based on its roundness or squareness, as well as how the characters break down space into dark and light areas.

If you have word processing or page layout software that supports kerning, the following list might provide some useful rules for applying kerning:

- Place the most amount of space around two characters composed of mostly vertical lines, such as *H* and *L*.

- Place less space between a vertical line letter and a curved letter, such as *H* and *O*.

- When two curves are placed side by side, they require very little spacing.

- When two letters produce large amounts of white space, place them close together. For instance, a diagonal line letter such as *A* can be placed very close to a vertical line letter such as *T*.

LEADING

Leading is the distance between the bottom of a line of text (including letters that swoop down such as *g*) and the top of the next line (including letters that swoop up such as *h*). Typesetters used to physically place pieces of lead between lines of type to make the type more legible. Today, the space between lines is called leading. The spaces between lines in a paragraph should always be consistent: 20 percent of the point size used in the paragraph. All auto-line spacing on Macintosh is set at 120 percent, or the point size plus 20 percent. When you increase the size of the font, the leading also increases automatically.

When you are typing in uppercase letters, the leading looks awkward because the letters lack descenders to break up the white space. Reset the leading to slightly less than the point size of the font to create the optical illusion that the spacing is 120 percent.

Use the Paragraph command in word processors or page-layout programs to adjust the spacing before and after paragraphs so that a few extra points will be added to the leading before and after a carriage return. The rule of thumb is to add half a line of space to the leading between paragraphs.

USING KEYCAPS

Just about every key on your keyboard (including the letter keys) can create four symbols, depending on which font is selected. The KeyCaps tool, distributed as part of Mac OS 8, provides a way for you to locate the keys you need to press to generate special symbols.

You can reach the KeyCaps feature from the Apple menu. When you select KeyCaps, a representation of the keyboard is displayed onscreen. The KeyCaps menu lists all the available character sets by font name. Selecting a font name causes the symbols from that font to display on the keyboard in the plain style. Figure 9.5 shows a standard KeyCaps window.

FIGURE 9.5   This is plain Palatino font in KeyCaps.

Pressing a modifier key (such as Shift, Option, and so on) displays the characters produced with that key to appear on the KeyCaps screen. For example:

- With no modifier key selected, pressing the 8 key on the keyboard produces the number 8.

- If you press the 8 key while holding down the Shift key, an asterisk (*) is produced.

- In most fonts, if you hold down the Option key while pressing the 8 key, a bullet symbol (•) is produced.

- Pressing the Option, Shift, and 8 keys at the same time produces a degree symbol (°).

> **Placing Symbols**   You need not open the KeyCaps screen to use a symbol listed in it; pressing the appropriate modifier and keyboard key (while in the proper font) is all you need to do to place a symbol in a document.

Some special characters remain consistent across fonts:

- Press Option+R to produce the ® mark.

- Press Option+2 to produce the ™ mark.

- Press Option+G to produce the © mark.

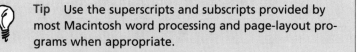

Tip   Use the superscripts and subscripts provided by most Macintosh word processing and page-layout programs when appropriate.

The Macintosh also provides a fraction bar to make fractional numbers easier to read. To make fractions even more elegant, do the following:

1. Press Option+! to produce the fraction bar; do not place a space between the whole number and the fraction.

2. Highlight the numerator in the fraction.

3. Apply Superscript to the numerator.

4. Adjust the denominator's size, making it two-thirds the point size of the original text.

5. If your software allows it, kern the numbers around the fraction bar.

Table 9.2 shows commonly used special characters and their keyboard positions.

TABLE 9.2   COMMON SPECIAL CHARACTERS

SPECIAL CHARACTER	KEYBOARD SHORTCUT
"	Option+[
"	Option+Shift+[
'	Option+]
'	Option+Shift+]
–	Option+-
—	Option+Shift+-
…	Option+;
•	Option+8
©	Option+G

SPECIAL CHARACTER	KEYBOARD SHORTCUT
®	Option+R
°	Option+Shift+8
¢	Option+4
/	Option+Shift+1
£	Option+3

This lesson discusses WYSIWYG, and then goes on to discuss how fonts are used on computers. You learned how to share fonts between computers, how to install fonts, how to view fonts, and how to add professional polish to your documents through the use of fonts.

LESSON 10
PRINTING

In this lesson you will learn how to set up and print from your iMac. You will also learn the difference between various printers and the benefits of using PostScript.

Before the advent of the Macintosh with its WYSIWYG environment and graphical user interface (GUI), displaying a document and printing it were two separate operations. Because the WYSIWYG screen display uses technologies similar to those used in printing a document, this is no longer true. QuickDraw guides both processes, ensuring that the text and graphics are drawn as specified.

The Macintosh was originally sold with a dot-matrix printer called the *ImageWriter*. In 1986, Apple replaced the first ImageWriter with an updated version called the *ImageWriter II*, which included a connection for sharing the printer over a network. As time progressed, users required a higher quality, faster, and quieter printing process for the Macintosh's graphics and text.

Vendors introduced laser printers that increased the quality of the output. These lasers used either Adobe's *PostScript* page description language to *rasterize* fonts, or more recently, used Macintosh's QuickDraw to rasterize their images. Vendors have also developed bridges to enable Macintosh to print on non-PostScript laser printers, thermal printers, and ink jet printers. Color QuickDraw and PostScript Level 2 have been used to enable Macs to print in color, as well. Lastly, the Macintosh also supports high-end electronic typesetters, such as Linotronics, to produce extremely high-quality (but expensive) printouts.

PRINTING WITH INKJET PRINTERS

Inkjet printers use tiny squirts of ink on pins to print dots on the page. Inkjet resolutions are better than dot-matrix printers, but most are not as good as laser printing resolutions. Although inkjet resolution averages

360dpi on best mode, Apple does manufacture a color inkjet that averages 720dpi in best mode for black-and-white text.

Most inkjet printers come bundled with Adobe Type Manager to rasterize Type 1 fonts on the Macintosh. They also come with their own set of outline fonts (Helvetica, Courier, Times, and Symbol), and can be upgraded to 35 or more resident fonts. Inkjets, like dot-matrix printers, receive rasterized images of TrueType fonts, which they use in conjunction with or in the place of their resident fonts. Inkjet printers are, therefore, not limited in their capability to print Adobe and TrueType fonts, because all of the hinting and scan conversion processes occur on the Macintosh.

 Rasterizing The process of converting EPS and outline font information into printable bitmapped images.

Their only limitation is that they do not support PostScript-based graphic formats, such as encapsulated PostScript, Adobe Illustrator, or Macromedia FreeHand graphics. You need a PostScript add-on card or interpreter to print PostScript graphics on an Inkjet printer. For example, InfoWave's StylePrint (`http://www.infowave.net/printing_solutions/html/ss_stylescript.html`) provides a software-based PostScript 2 emulator that lets you print PostScript files on inkjet printers.

Inkjets use special inks that tend to bleed on regular printer paper, although the technology is better today than when inkjets were first introduced in the late 1980s. Most vendors recommend printing on special coated papers made for inkjet printers when printing color images in best mode.

PRINTING WITH LASER PRINTERS

Laser printers produce output that is more capable of rendering the subtleties of electronic type as well as the details of a graphic drawing. This is because they print at a resolution of 1,200, 800, 600, or 300dpi versus the 144dpi of high-quality dot-matrix printers or the 720×360dpi of inkjets. Laser printing is also faster and quieter than dot-matrix printing.

Laser printers are more complex than dot-matrix printers because they use a laser to shine a light creating the dots on the page. The laser printer consists of an engine (a type of photocopier that manages the paper feeding and prints the image) and a controller (which accepts printing instructions from page description languages, such as PostScript or QuickDraw, and governs the engine following those routines).

USING POSTSCRIPT TO PRINT

PostScript is Adobe System's page description language. PostScript printers use controllers that reside in the printer's case. The controller is a computer, usually based on an RISC chip or Motorola CISC chips and using 2MB or more of random access memory (RAM), as well as read-only memory (ROM) chips containing the printer fonts stored in outline form.

When you send a document to the printer by selecting the Print command in your application program, the Macintosh Printer Manager checks to see whether there is a communications link to the printer.

The Mac OS downloads the custom PostScript Dictionary to the printer before the first use of the printer each time you turn it on. The PostScript Dictionary contains translations for QuickDraw's shorthand commands that speed up the printing process over AppleTalk networks. During the process of downloading, the desktop printer shows the message `Initializing Printer`. Only those portions of the PostScript Dictionary required to perform a specific print job are downloaded as needed. This also enables you to mix System 7 and System 8 versions of printer drivers on a network connected to the same printer.

BENEFITS OF POSTSCRIPT PRINTING

PostScript printers provide extensive benefits in terms of performance, cost savings, and flexibility. Because PostScript converts the QuickDraw code, the application program does not have to know the resolution of the printer you are using. You can, therefore, print on many different PostScript printers using the same file and application program. The difference is the quality of the output.

In addition, each bitmapped page takes up at least 1MB of memory. Because the controller performs the page processing, the page is stored in the printer's page buffer and not on the Macintosh, requiring less storage on the Macintosh to be dedicated to printing. Multiple Macs and personal computers can share one printer, because the PostScript and page buffer resides in the printer.

Each PostScript printer contains print server software in its ROM, allowing up to 32 machines to share the printer. The print server software acts as the interface between the Macintosh and the controller during the printing process. PostScript is a programming language, and as such can be upgraded and improved to provide extended features, such as shading, gradients, special effects, and other modifications to fonts and graphics.

PREPARING YOUR MAC FOR PRINTING

The iMac knows that there is a printer attached, but does not know how to send the proper instructions to that specific printer. You must do the following:

1. Set up your printer driver.

2. If you are printing with a PostScript printer, you must associate a PPD with the printer driver. If you are printing with a QuickDraw printer, you can set up who can share your printer using the Setup dialog box.

3. Select a default printer by clicking the appropriate USB port.

> **Printing with the iMac**   You can connect a LocalTalk printer, such as Apple's LaserWriters and all Hewlett-Packard DeskWriters, directly to the iMac by means of a LocalTalk-to-Ethernet adapter cable. Farallon (www.farallon.com) manufactures such a cable, called the iPrint.
>
> You can print from serial-port based printers, such as Epson's Stylus inkjets, other inkjets, or bubble jet printers using a USB-to-serial port adapter. Epson,
>
> *continues*

Keyspan, Momentum Inc., and Newer Technologies all offer such an adapter cable. You will need a USB printer driver for the inkjet printer to print or software such as Apple Printer Share (that comes with the StyleWriter series) or Stalker Software's PortSharePro. Epson is offering a free USB driver update for the Stylus 740 printer at www.epson.com.

SETTING UP YOUR PRINTER DRIVER

A *printer driver* is the intermediary that translates the QuickDraw commands used by the application to specify how a document should look into commands that can be used by a specific printer to print the document. These features, in turn, are displayed on the Page Setup and Print dialog boxes in all programs. Printer drivers are placed in the Extensions folder in the System Folder during the Mac OS installation process.

CHOOSING YOUR PRINTER'S PRINTER DRIVER

To select a printer driver, follow these steps:

1. Select the Chooser from the Apple menu.

2. In the Chooser, select your printer driver from the window on the left-hand side (see Figure 10.1).

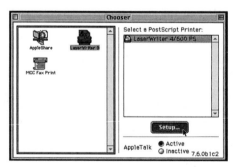

FIGURE 10.1   Use the Chooser to select a printer driver that matches your printer.

> **Which One?** Each driver is shown with its own icon representing its printer. If you don't know which printer you are using, try to match that printer's picture with the appropriate driver's icon.

3. When you select your driver, the right-hand list box displays one of several things.

   • If you are connected to a network, the box displays all the printers available for your use.

   • If you are running the printer directly from your iMac, the right-hand window displays the available USB port(s) for you to choose to locate your printer.

4. Select either a printer or a USB port.

5. Close the Chooser.

> **Print Drivers** Apple provides drivers only for its printers. You must go to your printer's manufacturer to obtain an up-to-date driver for your particular printer. Hewlett-Packard and Epson, being the only vendors still making printers for the Mac, maintain Web sites at www.hp.com and www.epson.com/home.html, respectively.

SETTING UP PRINTER DESCRIPTION DOCUMENTS

PostScript is a special page definition language that resides on your PostScript printer. Because PostScript is not resident on the iMac, the iMac needs some way to know about the specialized features of your PostScript printer. This information is provided by the PDD. You associate PDDs with your printer driver by selecting a printer driver from the Chooser and clicking Create. You can select the PDD that fits your printer using the resulting dialog boxes (see Figure 10.2).

> **Remember**   This task is required only if you are using PostScript. QuickDraw printers use the iMac's QuickDraw Toolbox manager to print, and so do not require these files.

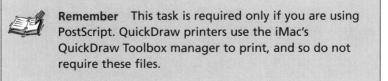

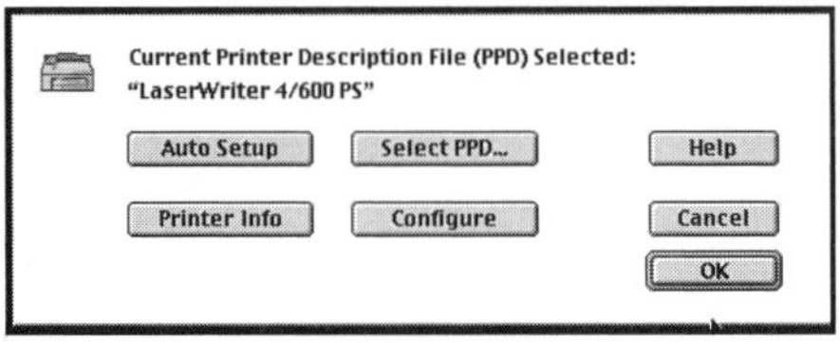

FIGURE **10.2**   Use the Printing Setup dialog box to select a PDD and configuration for your printer, or let the iMac set it up for you by clicking Auto Setup.

DESKTOP PRINTERS: SETTING THE DEFAULT PRINTER

Mac OS 8 introduced the concept of desktop printers. The iMac chooses a default printer and places its icon on the desktop. This printer will be the first one used when you print a document.

> **Be Careful When Selecting the Default Printer**   At this time, only Apple printers can be selected as the default printer. The default printer is selected when you run the Mac OS Setup Assistant (in the Assistants folder). Select an Apple printer from the list whether you are running an Apple printer or not. You can later throw away the printer's icon when it appears on your desktop. Apple has provided an Application Programming Interface (API) allowing non-Apple printers to set up desktop printers, but the printer vendors must rewrite their drivers to take advantage of this new Mac OS 8.5 function. So far, no vendor has done this.

By creating a desktop printer, Mac OS 8 lets you skip the step of going to the Chooser and picking a driver, printer, or serial port each time you want to print. You can set up default and alternative printers in a special menu on the menu bar using the desktop Printing menu's Default Printer command. The Printing menu appears when you select the desktop printer.

Assign the Default Printer   Mac OS 8 insists that there must be a default or desktop printer. The last printer you selected in the Chooser is this default.

After you create a desktop printer, its icon is placed on the desktop. You can then drag and drop documents from folders to the Printer icon to invoke their associated programs and print. You can place multiple files on the Printer icon, and they will be queued and printed using the priority you set in the Printing menu.

Stopping Print Jobs   You can stop or delete print jobs using the Printing menu. To see which documents are in the queue and check the status of your print jobs, double-click the desktop printer to open its Printing window (see Figure 10.3).

Ixchel			
‖ ► ⊙ ⬛			1 item
Default Printer
🖨	Untitled (print)
Status: processing job	Page: 1 of 1	Copies: 1
Name		**Pages**	**Copies**

FIGURE 10.3   The Printing window lets you view the status of your print jobs, as well as start, stop, and prioritize jobs.

PRINTING A DOCUMENT

The printer driver provides the Page Setup and Print dialog boxes used in the application program to initiate the printing process. There are two commands in every application that let you print using these tools:

- Page Setup

- Print

Both of these commands are typically located on the File menu.

USING PAGE SETUP

Page Setup provides options to tell the printer driver how you want your document pages formatted. You can set paper size (such as letter or legal size), a page's orientation (horizontal or vertical), and how large you want the view of the page to be (a reduction or enlargement factor). In addition, the Page Setup dialog box provides a way to set up special effects such as flipped views, inverted colors, and font handling options. Each program also adds its own specific options to the Page Setup dialog box.

Note that the Page Setup dialog box changes based on which printer driver you have selected in the Chooser. Because most people use either inkjet printers or PostScript laser printers, I'll focus this discussion on these two types of page setup screens. Figure 10.4 provides an illustration of the LaserWriter 8 Page Setup dialog box for Microsoft Word 6.

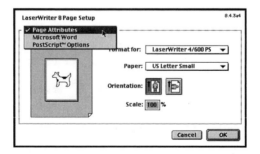

FIGURE 10.4   The LaserWriter 8 Page Setup dialog box lets you select the printer, the type of paper, the size of the image on the paper, and its orientation.

Selecting an item from the pop-up menu changes the dialog box from the default Page Attributes screen to a second screen called PostScript Options. This screen, shown in Figure 10.5, gives you the opportunity to choose from a number of special effects and printing correction options.

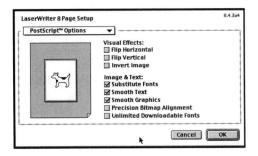

FIGURE 10.5   The PostScript Options screen lets you select special effects to correct certain problems with older printers.

Select the appropriate boxes to create the following PostScript effects:

- **Flip Horizontal** and **Flip Vertical**   Selecting either box creates a mirror image of your document. Use the Flip Horizontal option to change the image direction from right to left. This is useful if you are creating film images on a Linotronic typesetting, for transparencies, or if the pages have to be emulsion side down. Don't bother using Flip Vertical; you can always just turn the paper around.

- **Invert Image**   Checking this option reverses the colored areas of your document so that all white areas become black and vice versa. This option is useful if you are making negatives to use on a slide printer.

- **Substitute Fonts**   Checking this box replaces any fixed-size fonts (such as Geneva or New York) with their variable-size equivalents even if these latter fonts are not available. The side effect of this process is that word and sentence spacing is lost, because these spaces do not change even if you switch from fixed-size to variable-width fonts, making lines very jagged and hard to read. It is smart to leave this box unchecked.

- **Smooth Text**   Checking this box smoothes the jagged edges of fixed-size fonts for which there are no PostScript equivalents. The result is not always aesthetically pleasing. Leave this box unchecked. Always use variable-width fonts when printing.

- **Smooth Graphics**   Checking this box smoothes the jagged edges of bitmapped drawings, such as those produced by MacPaint, Painter, or any other bitmapped graphics program.

- **Precision Bitmap Alignment**   Checking this box corrects a problem that occurs because what you see onscreen is not necessarily what will be printed, especially when you are printing bitmapped graphics. This option reduces the entire printed image to enable the correct conversion of a 72dpi screen image to a 300 or 600dpi printed image (because 72 does not divide into 300 or 600 evenly). Reducing the image by four percent, effectively printing the image at 288 or 576dpi (an even multiple of 72dpi), aligns the bitmaps to produce a crisper output.

SETTING PAGE SETUP OPTIONS WITH THE STYLEWRITER

If you are using a StyleWriter, either the Color StyleWriter 1500 or 2500, or a StyleWriter II, selecting the appropriate printer driver in the Chooser presents a StyleWriter Page Setup dialog box, such as the Color StyleWriter Page Setup dialog box displayed in Figure 10.6.

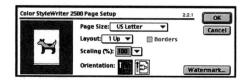

FIGURE 10.6   The StyleWriter provides fewer page setup options than those provided by the LaserWriter screen.

USING THE PRINT COMMAND

When you select the Print command from the File menu, a Print dialog box is displayed (the appearance of this dialog box might vary, depending on which printer driver you selected in the Chooser). Figure 10.7 shows the LaserWriter 8 Print dialog box.

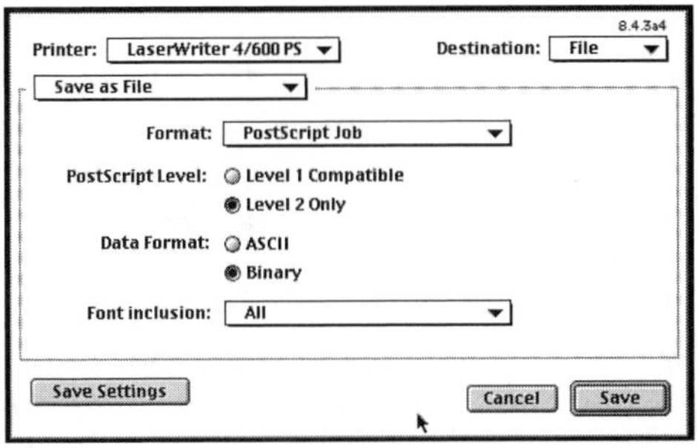

FIGURE 10.7   The LaserWriter Print dialog box lets you select which format to print in, which PostScript level to use, and which data format you want.

You can use the pop-up menu to select options for color management, error reporting, general printing (page numbers, copies, and so forth), and printing to a file. You can also choose to print a cover page for your document. In addition, you can save your print specifications so that the next time you want to print you can use one of your application's tools (such as a Print button or the ⌘+P keyboard shortcut).

PRINTING WITH COLOR

All color printers mix three or four pigments—cyan, magenta, and yellow and sometimes true black—to produce all other colors. These colors are the *primary* colors, and serve as the basis for all color printing. When all three colors are mixed equally, the result is a type of black, which is used as a fourth color. The resulting system is called *CMYK*, or *process color*.

Printers are categorized by how they apply their pigments; color printers can take several forms:

- They can use liquid or solid ink sprayed on the page (inkjet and phase change inkjet).

- They can use solid wax that is melted on a page (thermal wax).

- They can use pigments that are burned at different temperatures to produce the colors (dye sublimation).

ColorSync 2.5 Calibrates Color During Printing   Color printers use ColorSync to calibrate what you see on your monitor—which is displayed as combinations of red, green, and blue (RGB)—to how printers create colors with CMYK colors. The Print command allows you to use ColorSync 2.5 to ensure that your print colors match what you created onscreen. ColorSync 2.5 consists of three parts: a control panel where you set your RGB, CMYK, and Color Management default calibration files; the calibrator itself, which you set up in the Monitors & Colors control panel; and an API, which is used by vendors to allow their printer drivers' ColorSync to coordinate the various inputs to color printing.

This lesson covers printing with your iMac. The differences between types of printers were discussed, as were the benefits of using PostScript. You learned how to set up your iMac for printing, and how to print a document.

LESSON 11
COLOR

In this lesson you will learn about colors on your iMac, starting with a discussion about the differences between RGB and CMYK. You will also learn about ColorSync and ColorPicker, and learn how to calibrate colors on your iMac.

Designers know from years of experience that color commands attention. If you have a color manuscript, people are more likely to read what you have to say. Color advertisements are even more crucially important. The problem with color is that what you see onscreen is not necessarily what you get in your output. The capability to match what is displayed onscreen with what is outputted is called *color management*.

> **What You See Is Not Always What You Get** What is frustrating to designers is that the color space your eye can see is a lot broader than that which can be depicted on a computer monitor, scanned into your computer, or printed. Scientists call the spectrum that a device can accurately reproduce its *gamut*.

The development of algorithms and tables describing the available color spectrum (termed LAB colors) was a major breakthrough, because this measurement system provided a way to describe different coloring methods in a universal manner. *LAB color* is device-independent, meaning that it is not set to a particular printing or imaging technology. Color management is based on LAB colors.

WORKING WITH **RGB** AND **CMYK** COLORS

Let's look closer at color spaces. Monitors and scanners display colors using three basic hues: red, green, and blue (*RGB*). That is why displays are sometimes termed *RGB devices*. Every color displayed on a monitor or scanned into your computer is derived from red, green, or blue phosphors.

Printers and other output devices, however, create colors using a different color spectrum, sometimes called *process colors* because the spectrum is based on the ink colors cyan, magenta, yellow, and black. Process colors are also called *CMYK*.

Converting RGB and CMYK to LAB colors enables color-management software to correct and adjust colors in a unified way, allowing designers to use system-wide color management.

LAB color systems use *profiles* to describe the colors a device can convey. Profiles are dictionaries containing data on a specific device's color information. Every device comes from the factory with a color profile based on a scientific process called a *device characterization*. Profile information has been standardized through the work of the International Color Consortium (ICC). ICC profiles can be used across multiple computer platforms.

A CLOSER LOOK AT QUICKDRAW

QuickDraw converts all color profiles to RGB values for display, no matter what color model an application or device actually uses. QuickDraw sets up a coordinate plane—called the *hyperdesktop*—that identifies every pixel that can be drawn. Each pixel is divided into four axes that are given a color value: red, blue, or green (actually, this is communicated in the form of bit values from 0 to 65,535, providing a 16-bit number for each color) and a center point representing the color being displayed. The center point is described by a value for each axis representing the amounts of red, blue, and green the color contains. This composite number has a possible size of 48 bits.

In the RGB model, any color can be created by mixing red, green, and blue in different amounts. The more of each color you add, the closer to white you get; the fewer colors you add, the closer to black you get. The most colors you can combine is called the *white point*. The white point is important for calibrating your monitor and peripherals.

Every color identified by QuickDraw's hyperdesktop model is listed as a 48-bit RGB description in a System extension called *ColorPicker*.

QuickDraw uses the ColorPicker to see which color profile you have requested and looks up the closest approximation from the hardware's Color Manager toolbox and Graphics Device Manager toolbox's CLUT (color lookup table). The CLUT is a listing of every color your monitor or scanner can display described in 8-, 16-, or 32-bit numbers (depending on what you have set in your Monitors & Sounds control panel).

Here is where calibration comes in. When you have ColorSync 2.5 installed, you can calibrate your monitor to the Apple color-matching method (CMM) or any other CMM you have installed. ColorSync then matches how your input and output devices display colors, converting scanner RGBs to display RGBs to printer CMYK colors. ColorSync then attaches a color profile to each image for use by QuickDraw to manage color on the Mac.

COLOR-CALIBRATING YOUR MAC

Every iMac monitor comes with a preset color profile. You can adjust this profile using ColorSync 2.5 to fit your document production needs. To change the color profile, you use the ColorSync Monitor Calibration Assistant in the Monitors & Sound control panel.

MONITOR CALIBRATION ASSISTANT

The first task you need to do to calibrate your monitor is to adjust it physically so that it gives its best display. Do the following:

1. Open the Monitors & Sound control panel and click the Calibrate button (see Figure 11.1).

2. In the first screen of the Monitor Calibration Assistant, shown in Figure 11.2, you set your monitor's brightness and contrast. Push the appropriate buttons on your monitor to adjust these settings, using the assistant's interactive panel as your guide. If you can adjust the white point, alter that setting as well. When you are satisfied with these settings, click the right-arrow button at the bottom of the screen.

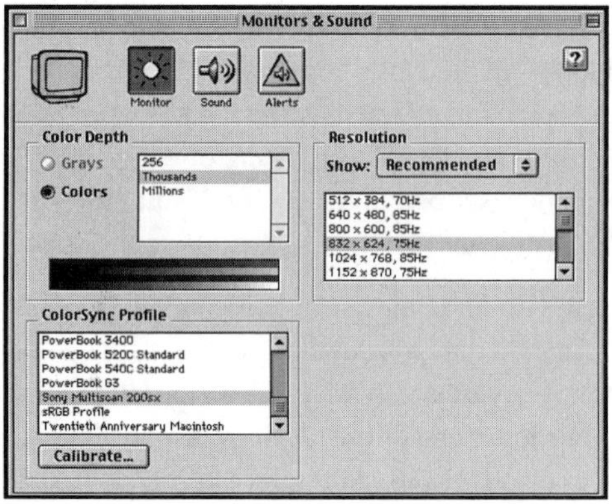

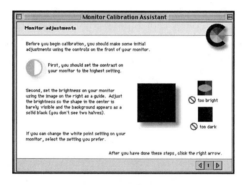

FIGURE 11.1   Click the Calibrate button on the Monitors screen of
the Monitor & Sound control panel to calibrate your monitor with
ColorSync.

FIGURE 11.2   Use the Monitor Calibration Assistant's first screen to
physically adjust the quality of your display.

3. Next, adjust the screen's *gamma*—the contrast between midtones
on your screen. Here, you are actually setting the density values
of the red, green, and blue colors that generate all your screen
colors. Use the sliders to adjust the colors until the apple in each
of the three windows is barely noticeable (see Figure 11.3).

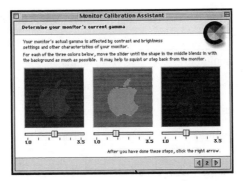

FIGURE 11.3   Adjust the midtone contrasts of your screen by using the sliders on this page.

4. In the next screen, shown in Figure 11.4, set a target gamma for your monitor. The target gamma is a way to define different brightness settings for different platforms. Table 11.1 illustrates how lightly or darkly different systems display the same picture. Select a radio button to change the gamma of your screen to represent different platforms. The preview window changes to show you the result of your choice.

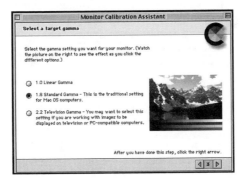

FIGURE 11.4   Adjust the brightness of your screen by selecting a target gamma.

TABLE 11.1   AVERAGE FACTORY SETTINGS FOR VARIOUS MONITORS

PLATFORM TYPE	GAMMA MEASUREMENT
Macintosh monitors	1.8 gamma
Silicon Graphics monitors	1.7 gamma
Intel PC monitors	2.5 gamma
Television monitors	2.2 gamma

 Go High or Go Low   The lower the target gamma is, the brighter the screen; the higher the target gamma is, the darker the screen.

5. In the next screen, select the color profile that best matches your monitor. For this screen, select the iMac monitor from the list.

6. The last screen, shown in Figure 11.5, adjusts the background whiteness of your display. You can approximate the light quality of your resulting document by adjusting the white point of your monitor. Click a radio button to see different white values.

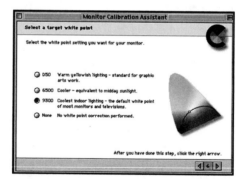

FIGURE 11.5   Choose a screen whiteness value from this page.

7. You have now calibrated your monitor to fit your design requirements; click Save to create a corrective profile and give that profile a name. This profile is used in the ColorSync 2 control panel
(it comes up as your default profile for your system when you
open the control panel).

CALIBRATING OTHER DEVICES

You use the ColorSync 2 control panel to set the corrective profiles for
your other input and output devices. Set the RGB profile to match your
system or select a profile from the list. The RGB selection lets you calibrate scanners and other input devices.

USING COLORPICKER

You can pick the color matching method (CMM) used by your application
in the ColorPicker to match its gamut to the RGB profile used by
QuickDraw. Figure 11.6 shows you the various CMM options in
ColorPicker. *ColorPicker* is a System extension that controls the CMM
used to convert colors from one device to another via ColorSync. All
applications that use color call on ColorPicker when you select a color (or
colors).

The quickest way to view ColorPicker is to select Other from the Colors
list for highlighting on the Appearance control panel (even though
ColorPicker operates in thebackground in many image processing and
graphics applications). The color selection formats for the ColorPicker
dialog box include the following:

- **CMYK Picker**   This enables you to select a color based on
cyan, magenta, yellow, and black (see Figure 11.6). Use this
CMM to choose colors that reflect those produced by printers
and other ink-based output devices. The color scale for each
color ranges from 0–100 percent. To create a color, move the
sliders across the four colors to create the desired highlight
color.

- **Crayon**   This presents a selected color range, applicable in any
color depth mode, using a crayon theme consisting of 60 colors
(see Figure 11.7). To change the highlight color, select any
crayon and click OK.

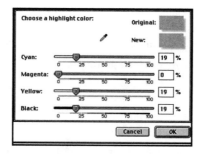

FIGURE 11.6   The CMYK ColorPicker dialog box.

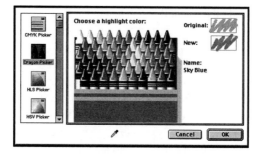

FIGURE 11.7   The Crayon ColorPicker dialog box.

- **HLS**   This presents the familiar color wheel from the original Color control panel (see Figure 11.8). The color wheel enables you to choose the highlight color. To select a color, click in the color wheel and adjust the slider bar below the wheel. The slider bar represents the lightness value to the right of the bar.

> **Create Your Own Color**   You can also create or adjust a color by using the values in the Hue Angle, Saturation, and Lightness fields. Hue Angle is measured in degrees (0–360), Saturation is a percentage (gray to 100 percent of the selected color), and Lightness is a percentage (ranging from black to white).

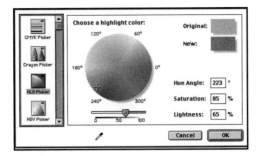

FIGURE 11.8   The Hue Angle, Lightness, and Saturation ColorPicker
dialog box.

- **HSV**   This enables you to select a color from settings similar to
  HLS. The *V* in HSV stands for *value*, which is reflected both in
  the slider bar and in the Value field, and is a percentage ranging
  from black to 100 percent of the pure selected color. Hue Angle
  and Saturation are also measured here, as in the HLS dialog box.

- **HTML**   This consists of red, green, and blue slider bars with
  an HTML value in the lower-right corner of the window (see
  Figure 11.9. Use this CMM if you want to choose colors that
  represent those that a browser can use. This CMM is very useful
  when you are creating Web pages because you can visualize the
  color represented by its hexadecimal code. Each slider bar is fol-
  lowed by a text field that converts the color value to an HTML
  color value. Settings for each color range from 00–FF. You can
  also input an HTML value into the HTML field, and the RGB
  sliders will reconfigure to show the input value's color.

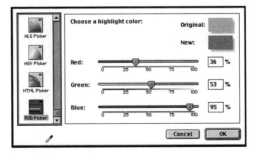

FIGURE 11.9   The HTML ColorPicker dialog box.

- **RGB**   This enables you to select a red, green, or blue value to
  create the highlight color (see Figure 11.10). Each color is fol-
  lowed by a Value field showing the percentage of that color used
  to create the highlight color. All slider bars share a scale starting
  from zero, and moving up 25 notches to 100.

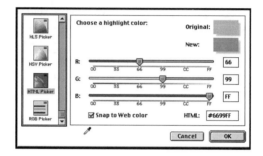

FIGURE **11.10**   The RGB ColorPicker dialog box.

OTHER USES OF COLORSYNC

ColorSync 2.5 also includes a plug-in that you can drag into your image
processing or graphics applications' Plug-ins folder. This is the physical
manifestation of ColorSync. When you install the ColorSync plug-in,
ColorSync takes over the task of matching filters, color separations, pre-
views, and output colors in that application. Figure 11.11 shows an example of ColorSync in action, performing color separation (splitting out the
layers of cyan, magenta, yellow, and black into separate documents) for
pre-press use.

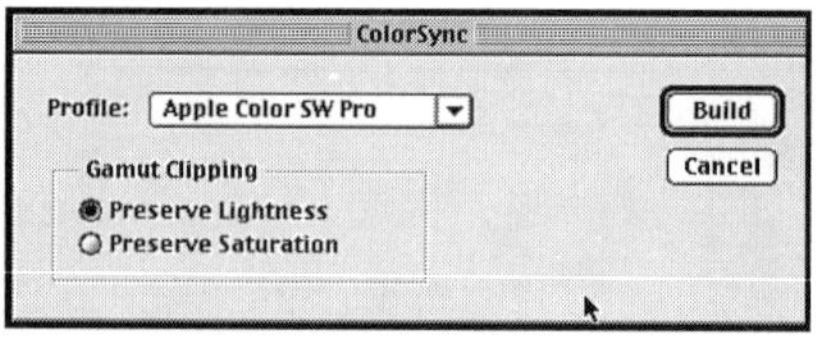

FIGURE **11.11**   PhotoShop uses the ColorSync plug-in to manage
color-separate tasks.

Review Your Manuals   Read the documentation from your image-processing application for more information on how to use ColorSync with that software.

This lesson discussed the use of colors on your iMac, starting with a discussion of the difference between RGB and CMYK colors. You learned about QuickDraw, and then you learned to color-calibrate your iMac. Finally, you learned about ColorPicker and ColorSync.

LESSON 12
QUICKTIME

In this lesson you will learn how to set QuickTime preferences, work with QuickTime-savvy programs, and use the QuickTime plug-in.

You've seen QuickTime in action if you have played Broderbund's Myst or Riven, used Microsoft Encarta, or played Id Software's Doom II. QuickTime enables your iMac to integrate text, still graphics, video, animation, 3D, virtual reality (VR), and sound into a cohesive whole. QuickTime has become the foundation in many video editing and multimedia creation programs for the production of video and audio documents. In addition, QuickTime provides the means to transmit and play real-time digital video over the Internet.

QuickTime is not a single program, but a technology consisting of a host of small component programs that together provide digital video production and display. QuickTime resides on the iMac as a whole series of system extensions that enable the different pieces of the architecture, including QuickTime VR, QuickDraw 3D, QuickTime Plug-in, QuickTime MPEG, and CODEC files, to function. The visible portion of the technology consists of two applications for viewing pieces of QuickTime: MoviePlayer and PictureViewer. In addition, QuickTime 3.0 includes a plug-in for Netscape Navigator and Microsoft Internet Explorer to let you view streaming video in real-time on the Internet.

The latest version of QuickTime, QuickTime 3.0, is included in Mac OS 8.5.

QuickTime 3.0 provides the following benefits:

- It is one of the technology standards for delivery and playback of CD-ROM and Internet content on many platforms.

- It supports multiple data types—for example multiple-language text tracks, video, sound, graphics, animation, text, music/MIDI, sprites, 3D, and virtual reality.

- If you upgrade to QuickTime Pro, you can use your Mac to create video productions—including hybrid Windows/Mac CDs—that can be played back on most platforms.

- Creation of videos is made easier because QuickTime provides advanced tools, such as the automatic synchronization of sound, video, music, and other data tracks to a common time base.

QuickTime There are two flavors of QuickTime: QuickTime 3.0, a free set of tools to play QuickTime media; and QuickTime Pro, a software package that lets you create QuickTime applications. QuickTime Pro is a more robust version that lets you actually construct videos. You'll find when you first open QuickTime 3.0 that Apple places innumerable ads asking if you want to purchase the upgrade for $29.95.

USING QUICKTIME

Using QuickTime is almost a no-brainer because applications do most of the work for you. QuickTime is a technology; that is, it provides functionality to applications rather than being an application itself. You need an application to view QuickTime-based video or image data. Playback is supported by games, Web sites, and any other software that uses video, such as encyclopedias spanning a range of features, from authoring video, sound, and animation, to playing back all these multimedia elements.

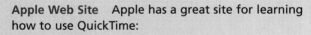 **Apple Web Site** Apple has a great site for learning how to use QuickTime:

http://www.apple.com/quicktime/information/

SETTING QUICKTIME PREFERENCES

Use the QuickTime Settings control panel to select which features of QuickTime you want to run as well as how you want the technology to behave. This control panel contains six distinct sections:

- AutoPlay

- Connection Speed

- Media Keys

- Music

- QuickTime Exchange

- Registration

Through these settings panels, you can control the transmission speed of incoming and outgoing video and audio signals, access secure media files, translate foreign media files into QuickTime-playable files on-the-fly, and manage how QuickTime replays video and audio.

SETTING AUTOPLAY PREFERENCES

If the AutoPlay feature is enabled, audio CDs and CD-ROMs are started automatically when they are inserted into the computer (see Figure 12.1). With AutoPlay, audio CDs automatically start with Track 1.

Playing CDs   Even if you've enabled AutoPlay for audio CDs, you can still use the Apple Audio CD Player or a similar application to control audio CD playback. Simply launch that application before inserting the CD.

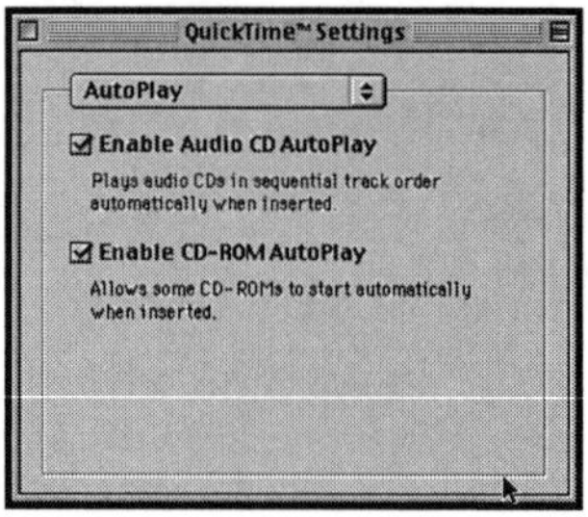

FIGURE **12.1**   The AutoPlay section of the QuickTime Settings control panel.

SETTING CONNECTION SPEED

The speed of your modem has a great impact on the quality of QuickTime movies you play back from the Internet. Use the Connection Speed screen in the QuickTime Settings control panel (see Figure 12.2) to tell QuickTime the best performance your modem is capable of providing; in this case because the iMac comes with a built-in 56Kbps modem, use the 56Kb to T1 setting. QuickTime adjusts its streaming video to accommodate your requirements.

FIGURE 12.2   The Connection Speed section lets you tell QuickTime how fast your modem can transmit data.

SETTING MEDIA KEYS

The Media Keys screen of the QuickTime Settings control panel (shown in Figure 12.3) is rather obscure; you use this screen to set up password keys that are used to access proprietary or private servers.

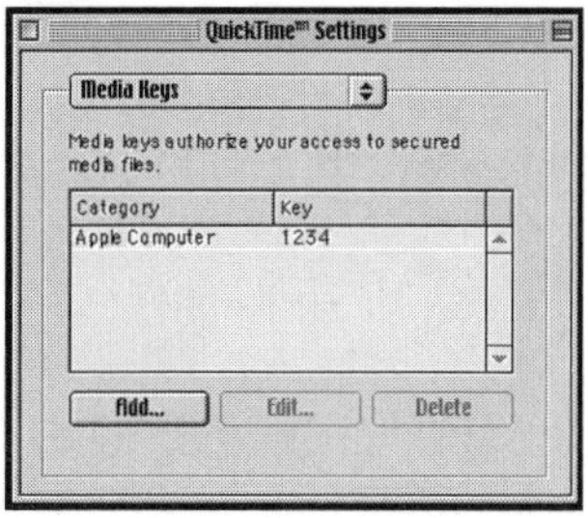

FIGURE 12.3   Use the Media Keys panel to list passwords used to access private or secure servers containing video files.

SETTING MUSIC PREFERENCES

Use the Music screen in the QuickTime Settings control panel to select the default music synthesizer for QuickTime to use.

> **QuickTime and MIDI**   QuickTime Music Synthesizer is the default setting for the control panel unless MIDI hardware or other music-related hardware is connected to the computer.

SETTING UP QUICKTIME EXCHANGE

Multimedia on computers is currently a Tower of Babel with every digital video device maker creating its own proprietary video formats. Luckily, QuickTime can import foreign formats and work with them, provided you enable Exchange using the check box in the QuickTime Exchange screen of the QuickTime Settings control panel (see Figure 12.4).

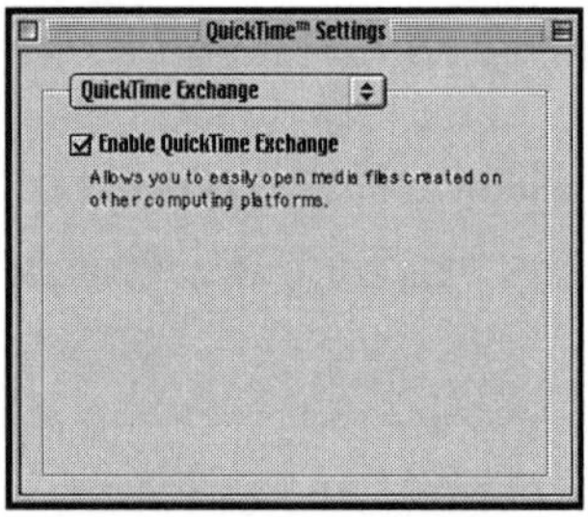

FIGURE 12.4   Use the QuickTime Exchange screen to configure QuickTime to import, work with, and export non-QuickTime video file types.

REGISTRATION

If you want to upgrade to QuickTime 3.0 Pro, use the Registration screen to enter the decryption code provided by Apple when you pay your $29.95. Selecting Registration while your ISP is online automatically jumps you to the www.quicktime.apple.com site where you can upgrade your QuickTime. After inserting the code, QuickTime Pro is unlocked on your iMac.

WORKING WITH QUICKTIME-SAVVY PROGRAMS

You need a player or application to be able to view QuickTime video. Apple provides MoviePlayer, but many games, encyclopedia programs, browsers, and word processing/layout programs also provide the capability to play QuickTime files. The following sections describe how to play QuickTime on such applications.

MOVIEPLAYER

MoviePlayer automatically opens when you double-click a QuickTime movie icon (see Figure 12.5).

 QuickTime Movies MoviePlayer prefers 2MB of memory in order to support playback of QuickTime movies.

FIGURE 12.5   MoviePlayer automatically opens when you double-click a QuickTime movie icon.

Another way to play a movie is to first open the MovieMaker application, and select the movie from there:

1. Double-click the MovieMaker icon (located in the QuickTime 3.0 folder installed with Mac OS 8.5).

2. Choose Open from the File menu.

3. Click Open.

4. The QuickTime screen is displayed and the movie plays.

USING MOVIEPLAYER CONTROLS

MoviePlayer consists of many of QuickTime's standard interface features, such as the controller with its slider and button controls. This controller, shown in Figure 12.6, lets you choose audio and video playback settings with a mouse click.

To operate the controller interface, do the following:

1. Press the Spacebar or click the Play button to play back the movie.

2. Adjust the sound using the Sound volume button.

3. During playback, you can click the arrow keys to step a frame forward or backward.

4. During playback, you can click anywhere on the slider bar to jump to a different location in the movie file.

Sound
volume ⌐   ⌐ Play   Fast forward ⌐   ⌐ Rewind

FIGURE 12.6   The MoviePlayer controller.

MoviePlayer Features   MoviePlayer also has import, export, track editing, and window size controls for any image-based movie file.

Using Zoom   Smaller window sizes provide more optimal performance than large window sizes. Use the movie window's standard zoom box to drag the window larger or smaller.

PLAYING AUDIO FILES WITH MOVIEPLAYER

MoviePlayer can play back audio-only sound files, as well as single- or multi-track audio and video movie files. Opening a sound file with MoviePlayer brings up an Open dialog box as well as a dialog box asking where to save the QuickTime audio file. The controller for audio-only playback looks and works the same as with a movie file, except no image window area is visible. The controller allows you to play back part or all of the audio clip.

MoviePlayer also provides these additional features:

• Video compression—There are several image and audio compression codecs in QuickTime that provide differing levels of output for video compression. Almost all compression methods shrink the amount of disk space used to store the video and audio data.

• You can change controllers.

• You can add video or audio tracks from other movies.

• You can use drag and drop to add animation, graphics, or video to a movie file.

PLAYING BACK MOVIES IN OTHER PROGRAMS

Any application that supports QuickTime (such applications are called *QuickTime-savvy*) can be used to play back a video. For example, SimpleText, the text editor that comes with Mac OS 8.5, is QuickTime-savvy and as such can be used to play back movies. Click the movie window in the application to play the movie.

> **Setting Preferred Memory** SimpleText's preferred memory is set to 512KB. However, if you plan on using it for movie playback, it is recommended to increase the preferred memory size to 2MB. If SimpleText does not have enough memory to open a particular movie file, it indicates this by showing a message dialog box.

Opening a QuickTime movie with a savvy program such as SimpleText brings up the same window and set of controls as MoviePlayer, but with a smaller set of menus (the player lacks the loop and track menu features in MoviePlayer, but does support file import and export).

> **Converting Files**   Both MoviePlayer and SimpleText let you open a standard MIDI file and convert it into a QuickTime music track. You can also use either application to convert the MIDI file and save it as a QuickTime movie. After the file is saved, the music can be played back using the controller.

SAVING A VIDEO IN THE SCRAPBOOK

Suppose you find a royalty-free movie on the Web that you want to copy into a document. You can save the movie in the Scrapbook, where you can access it from any application on your iMac. Audio-only, or video and audio movies, can be moved to the Scrapbook a couple of different ways:

- You can move an entire movie out of MoviePlayer into the Scrapbook by dragging and dropping the open movie window into the Scrapbook window.

- The audio or image files can be copied and pasted into the Scrapbook.

After the image is in the Scrapbook, all the QuickTime controls for sound volume and playback become available in the Scrapbook window (editing movies is not supported). The Scrapbook displays the duration and dimensions of the QuickTime movie—as well as the movie's file size—in its main window. The window size of the movie is scaled to fit into the Scrapbook, and will not reflect the of image quality if played back in MoviePlayer.

USING PICTUREVIEWER

QuickTime 3.0 introduced a new way to draw still images using its PictureViewer Pro application. Graphics importer components within PictureViewer provide a standard method to open and display still images from any type of image data, regardless of the file format or compression used in the document. You specify the document that contains the image, and the destination rectangle the image should be drawn into, and QuickTime handles the rest. The PictureViewer application in QuickTime Pro lets you manipulate these still images before placing them into a movie.

WORKING WITH THE QUICKTIME PLUG-IN

One of the most beneficial components of the QuickTime 3.0 package is the inclusion of a new QuickTime plug-in for Web browsers. QuickTime Plug-in 2.0 contains expanded browser support for Netscape Navigator 4.0, Internet Explorer for Macintosh 4.0, and for Windows 9*x*/NT, letting you view just about any video or audio media type or file format with a single viewer.

To use the QuickTime plug-in, you have to copy it into the Plug-ins folder with your browser. Then, whenever you start your browser, it initiates the QuickTime plug-in along with its other plug-ins to enable you to download streaming video. The following is a list of other new features included with QuickTime Plug-in 2.0:

- *Scaled Movies*—This feature allows movies to play back at different sizes.

- *Cached Movies*—This feature (for Netscape 4.0 users only) caches movies you have recently viewed so they don't need to be reloaded when you return to them.

- *Expanded media type Fast Start support*—This feature lets you configure your browser to use the Apple QuickTime plug-in to play non-QuickTime files such as AIFF audio files.

- *MPEG playback support*—This is provided via the QuickTime MPEG extension.

- *QTVR Hot Spots with embedded URL data*—"Hot spots" in a QTVR movie can have URL data associated with them, enabling them to load new pages or media when they are clicked. (Requires QTVR Authoring Studio to create new URL hot spots with VR 2.1.)

- *Expanded media type support for both Macintosh and Windows*—You can configure your browser to use the QuickTime plug-in to play non-QuickTime files such as WAV audio files. QuickTime 3.0 now supports playback of nearly 20 different media types!

- *Full-feature parity*—With QuickTime 3.0 for Windows, you can have full-feature parity across Windows 95, Windows NT, and MacOS.

- *Pop-up menus*—Pop-up menus are always available for visible movies—even sound-only movies.

- *Capability to disable playback of selected MIME types.*

- *Expanded Save options*—You can save a file as its original file type (such as AIFF) rather than as a movie.

- *Drag and drop*—You can drag and drop a movie to the desktop.

- *Support for QuickTime VR 2.1.*

- *Support for the QuickTime 3.0 URL-linking feature.*

Unfortunately, the new QuickTime plug-in (Version 2.0) has removed the capability to save movies from the Web. In order to use a browser's Save Movie context menu command, you must purchase the Pro key and upgrade to QuickTime Pro. The professional version of QuickTime upgrades the plug-in, restoring the capability that was standard in the Version 1.1 plug-in.

In this lesson, you learned how to set QuickTime preferences, how to work with QuickTime-savvy programs, and how to use the QuickTime plug-in.

LESSON 13

BROWSING WITH THE IMAC

In this lesson you will learn how to get connected to the Internet to surf, chat, send email, and participate in newsgroups.

So, what's all this jive about Webs, surfers, highways, and such got to do with Macintosh? In a word: everything. The Internet provides interactive communications in the form of email, telephony, published documents, and avenues to gain direct access to software and information. This is the Information Superhighway.

GAINING ACCESS

The iMac was built to surf. The computer is optimized for communicating and its software provides easy access to the Internet in any of three ways.

- Use an Internet service provider (ISP).

- Join a commercial online service that provides gateways or a door to the Web.

- Use a corporate server.

INTERNET SERVICE PROVIDERS

ISPs offer relatively cheap access to the Internet. Typically, an ISP provides you with a server address that you can dial in to using a local telephone number (called a *Point of Presence [POP]* connection). This is your conduit on to the Internet. You can use the software typically provided by the ISP.

ISPs are proliferating and consolidating. Local telephone companies, long-distance carriers such as AT&T and MCI, entertainment conglomerates such as Time-Warner, and former video rental operators such as Erols are all getting into the ISP business. National companies such as EarthLink, Netcom, and MacLink offer an extensive array of Internet connection services at escalating prices based on the speed and size of the connection.

ISPs typically charge a flat monthly fee. Due to the unprecedented (they really should have known) growth in Internet use both in length of a session and how many people are logging on to the Internet, flat, one-size-fits-all monthly fees are giving way to escalating fee structures based on the quantity and quality of access required. What do you get for your monthly access fee as a single user? Most ISPs offer an email address, connection to the Internet via an Internet address, 1 or 2MB of space (or more) for personal home pages, and possibly space for uploading files for FTP serving.

> **Ensuring Point of Presence**   Make sure that your ISP offers a local POP so that you do not have to pay long-distance telephone rates on top of the monthly Internet access rate for your browsing and site managing. If you live near a metropolitan area, there should be a local telephone number available.

COMMERCIAL ONLINE SERVICES

Commercial online services, such as America Online (AOL) and its subsidiary, CompuServe, offer gateways to the Internet as well as other features such as chat rooms, email, newsgroups, and more. Apple makes it very easy to use AOL; AOL's software (version 3.0) is included with the iMac.

> **iMac and AOL**   iMac.5 does not include AOL software, but just about every magazine about Macs does include an AOL CD-ROM. This section focuses on AOL because it is the most Mac-friendly commercial online service.

AOL

AOL works great if you are interested in obtaining small snippets of information about a topic, or have only a few emails to send or receive daily. AOL provides connections to many software companies, entertainment sites, shopping sites, travel links, and chat rooms.

AOL can be accessed in two ways:

- Via AOLLink, AOL's TCP/IP software, which AOL installs in your Extensions folder.

- Via Open Transport/Apple Remote Access (ARA) if you have set up an ISP account.

AOLLink If you have iMac's ARA upgrade and an ISP account, AOLLink will not work. You can install AOL with Open Transport by not using AOLLink and connecting to AOL via your Remote Access software, as described later in this chapter.

In either case, do the following:

1. Click the Setup button on AOL's Welcome dialog box.

2. Select TCP as your connection method in the resulting Setup dialog box, shown in Figure 13.1.

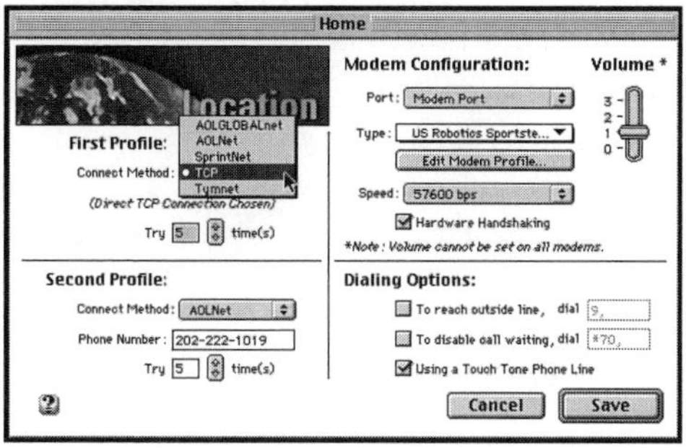

FIGURE **13.1** Use the Setup dialog box to use ARA and your ISP account to link to AOL.

AOL uses a modified version of Microsoft Internet Explorer (Figure 13.2) that lacks a mail tool (thankfully, AOL has its own mail software built in) as well as some of the commercial browser's other bells and whistles (built-in search engines, a robust bookmark system, and so forth). You can still use Netscape or the commercial version of Internet Explorer in addition to using AOL.

FIGURE **13.2**   AOL's browser is a rudimentary version of Microsoft Internet Explorer.

AOL is divided into various topic areas, called *channels*. Each channel provides newsgroup forums as well as links to selected Web sites related to that channel's topic area. AOL also provides message boards for discussion, as well as access to Internet newsgroups. AOL offers many special interest groups, services, and magazines (e-commerce is alive and well on AOL). If you're not sure which channel contains the information you're looking for, fear not. AOL offers an extensive array of search engines via its Web page: http://www.aol.com.

Limitations of AOL   The AOL service offers limited information on topics; only vendors who have signed up with AOL are featured on AOL's pages. For example, *MacWorld* retains a presence on AOL, whereas *MacWeek* does not. If you are looking for articles appearing in *MacWeek*, you must link to the Web using the Internet channel's World Wide Web area. Type an URL in the text box (in this example, http://www.zdnet.com/macweek), click the Go to the Web button, and AOL takes you to the specified site.

Are You Ready for an ISP?   When you find yourself linking to the Web more than you are using AOL's channels, you probably are outgrowing AOL and ready to move up to the grown-up world of ISPs.

CORPORATE SERVERS

Many large companies and most universities offer access to the Internet over very fast leased telephone lines (called T1 lines). Users in these environments can connect to the Internet from their desks using their organization's local area network (LAN) and server. The downside of this free access is that users must go through their computer operations or MIS department to gain access and permission to maintain a Web site. Often they are limited in the access they are accorded to the server.

GETTING ON THE INTERNET

When you first turn on your iMac and run the Macintosh Setup Assistant the next assistant that pops up is the Internet Setup Assistant. This powerful program gets you set up with your existing ISP, EarthLink (Apple's ISP of choice), or any other new ISP you might want to use. Answer the series of questions the iMac asks, and you are on your way:

1. *Would you like to set up your computer to use the Internet?*
   Click No to abort the Internet Setup Assistant process; click Yes to advance to the next screen.

2. *Do you already have an Internet account?* If you click No, Setup Assistant assists you in finding an ISP with POPs in your area. This portion of the Internet Setup Assistant is called the ISP Referral Assistant. If you click Yes, Setup Assistant enables you to add the iMac to your existing account.

USING THE ISP REFERRAL ASSISTANT

Apple selected EarthLink as its ISP of choice because this ISP provides POP connections nationwide, is relatively Mac-friendly, and has an excellent customer service reputation. When you invoke the ISP Referral Assistant, the following occurs:

1. You are connected to the Apple Referral Server for your area code and telephone exchange.

2. Apple retrieves the EarthLink POP closest to your area and dials into EarthLink's server.

3. Internet Explorer is opened to the EarthLink/Sprint setup page.

Follow the instructions on this page to set up an EarthLink account. At this time, you'll choose a username and password. You need to enter a credit card number to complete the transaction (the server is secure, so you can safely transmit this information to EarthLink). When you have completed the application, EarthLink automatically runs Total Access to set up the iMac for your new account.

Finding an ISP   The Internet Setup Assistant can't help you find your own ISP. So if you do not currently have an ISP but do not want to join EarthLink, you're on your own. After you've signed up with an ISP, you can use the Internet Setup Assistant to add your iMac to the ISP account and to configure the connection (see the next section).

USING INTERNET SETUP ASSISTANT TO ADD THE iMAC TO YOUR ISP ACCOUNT

When you indicate that you want to use your existing ISP, iMac directs you to the portion of the Internet Setup Assistant used for configuring ISP accounts.

> **Running the Provided Software**   Typically, if you run the software provided by your ISP, such as Netcom's NetComplete, you will have already configured the iMac and the assistant will have the information it requires.

If you are reinstalling your Internet connection after a crashed system, you'll need the following information (ask your ISP or system administrator):

- The telephone number of your local connection. This is sometimes called a *POP* or *dial-in number.*

- Your username (also called your *user ID* or *login name*) and password. Without these two pieces of information, you cannot access your ISP's server or the Internet. These are the first pieces of information your ISP will set when you open an account. Don't lose them.

- The name of the ISP's domain. (Ask your ISP for this information.)

- The numeric name of your ISP's server(s). This is called the DNS (*domain name server*) or router address and is very important for ensuring that you connect to the right server. (Ask your ISP for this information.)

- The name of the incoming mail or POP server. This is your email server. The name consists of the server's domain and POP identification. Netcom's is popd.ix.netcom.com.

- The name of the outgoing mail server or SMTP server. This is the server that handles the delivery of email and attachments. (Ask your ISP for this information.)

- Your email address. This is typically your user ID joined to the ISP's domain name by an @ symbol.

- If you are interested in joining any Usenet newsgroups you need to know the newsgroup's domain name. This is typically the name of the newsgroup server and your ISP's domain name.

- You might need to know your PPP server name. (Check with your ISP for this information.)

The input of this information begins on screen 6, shown in Figure 13.3. Here, you must type your username, password, and the telephone number for the local connection to your ISP. Be sure to add area codes.

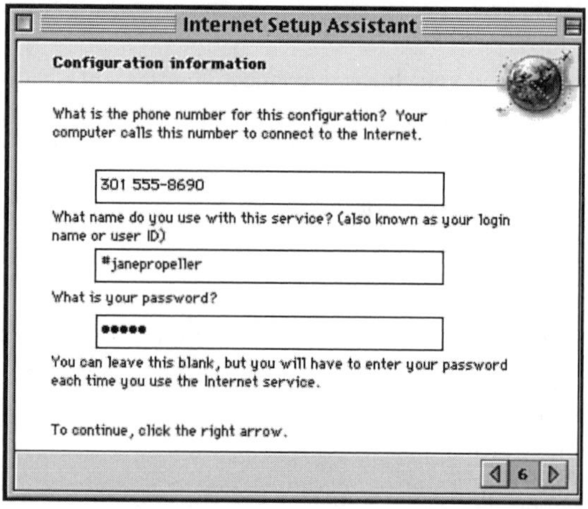

Figure **13.3**   Enter the local telephone number for your ISP.

Screen 10, shown in Figure 13.4, is where you get to the nitty-gritty of configuring TCP/IP. Carefully type the router address for your ISP. (These are the four-part numbers mentioned earlier.)

Ensuring the Proper Domain Name   The Internet Setup Assistant checks for the proper number of numbers, proper period placements, and so forth to ensure that you get the information correct. If you get any of these wrong, the assistant asks you to re-enter the number.

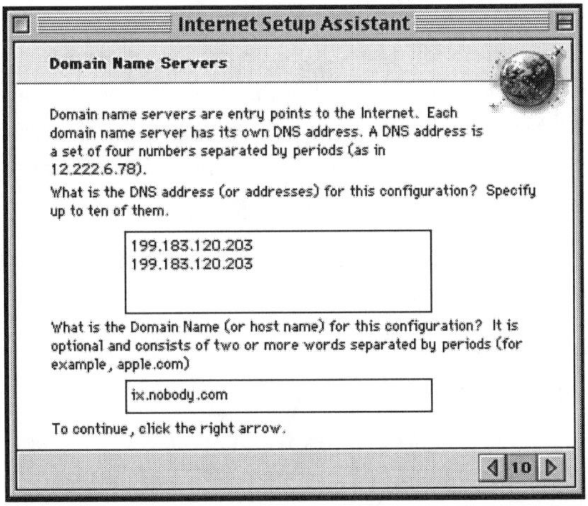

FIGURE 13.4   Type the domain name server number(s) in the box.

There are two more items to complete:

- You need to set up your email account(s). Figure 13.5 shows the screen used to set up your email.

- You need to point your browser at your newsgroup address.

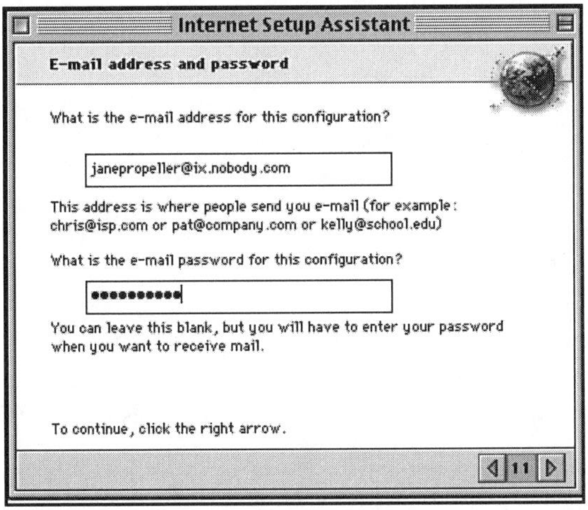

FIGURE 13.5   Fill in the text boxes with your email domain names and email ID.

If you want to ensure that the information you entered is correct, click the
Overview button on screen 14 to display a review of your configuration.
You can go back and change anything that is wrong or incomplete.
(Actually, the Assistant is so smart that it prompts you to correct overtly
wrong information.) Click Go Ahead to prompt the Assistant to automati-
cally complete four control panels:

* Modem   Tells the iMac the capabilities of your modem (see
  Figure 13.6)

* Remote Access   Tells the iMac information about your connections to the Internet.

* TCP/IP   Tells the iMac information about the Internet (see
  Figure 13.7).

* Internet   Replaces Internet Config as the repository of your
  Internet preferences.

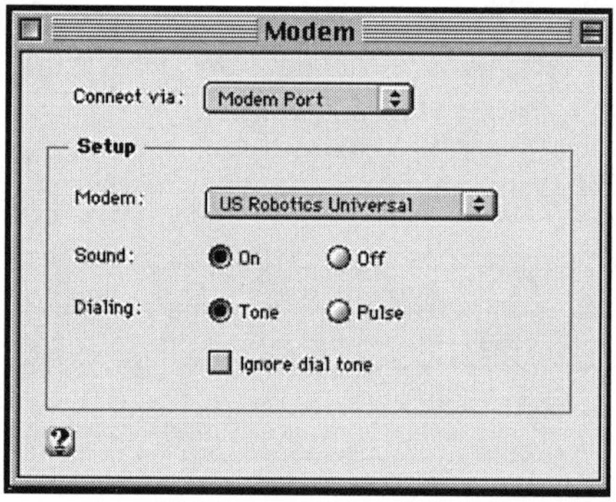

FIGURE **13.6** The Modem control panel tells the iMac the capabilities of your modem.

When you are finished, you can open each panel to ensure that the data
has been entered correctly. You can also change these panels individually
(although be careful because one wrong number messes up all four panels).

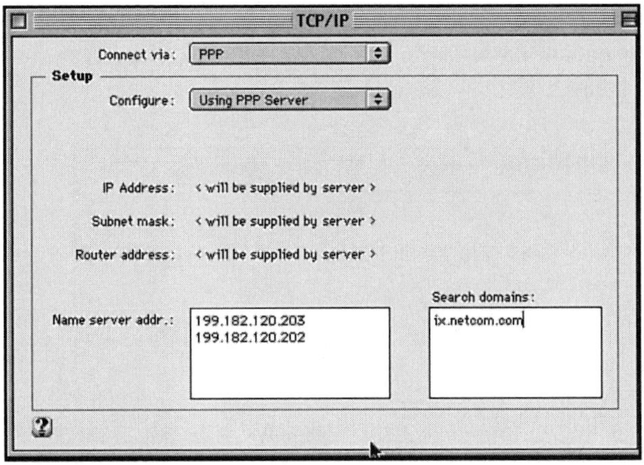

FIGURE 13.7   The TCP/IP control panel tells the iMac information about the Internet.

CONFIGURING YOUR INTERNET PREFERENCES

Apple has provided a control panel called Internet—a version of the venerable Internet Config—that makes your life easier (see Figure 13.8). Use the Internet control panel to select preferences for different parts of your Web browsing experience, including home page, email, newsgroups, and general settings. You can group your settings under a name (called a *set*). Using sets allows you to switch configurations to fit your browser and browsing requirements by selecting a new set from the Active Set pop-up menu.

WORKING WITH CONFIGURATION SETS

With the Internet control panel open you can activate, edit, rename, and remove sets of configurations.

- Activate another configuration set by selecting a name from the Active Set pop-up menu.

- Create a new set of configurations by selecting Untitled from the Edit Sets pop-up menu. Enter the information requested on each tab and make your preference selections. When you are done, select Rename from the File menu. In the resulting dialog box, type a new name in the text box and click Rename. You can use this command to rename existing sets as well.

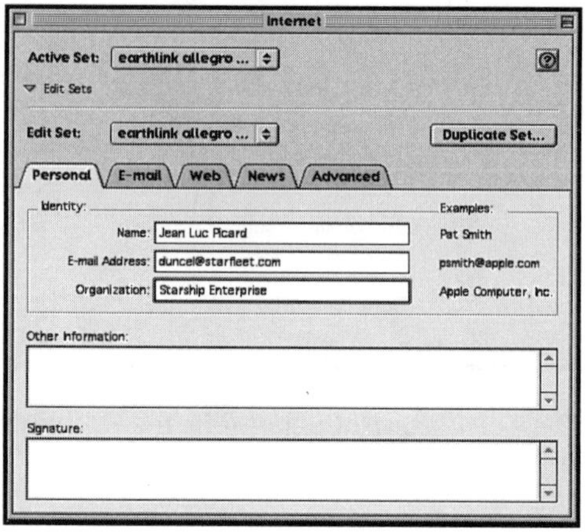

FIGURE 13.8   Use the Internet control panel to select various preferences.

- Duplicate an existing set to make slightly different configuration settings by selecting an existing set from the Edit Sets pop-up menu and clicking the Duplicate button. Make sure that the copy is selected in the Edit Sets menu and make your changes.

- Delete a set by making sure that the unwanted set is not active or in the Edit mode and selecting Delete from the File menu. In the resulting Delete dialog box, select the set you want to delete and click Delete.

- Save a set by closing the control panel. Your changes are always saved prior to quitting the Internet control panel.

WORKING WITH THE PERSONAL INFORMATION TAB

When you use the Internet Setup Assistant to set up your Internet system on iMac, the information about your user ID, password, company name, username, and email information is automatically entered into the Internet control panel. The Personal tab contains data about your username, ID, password, and company name. In addition, you can add a signature to your name by typing a message in the Signature text box. Signatures are fun ways to tell a little about yourself (whether it's a personal Web site, a publications list, a favorite quote, or a telephone number). Signatures are included in emails that you send when you select Internet Config as your configuration manager in your browser.

THE EMAIL TAB

Information in your Email tab is automatically entered for you when you set up your Internet connection (see Figure 13.9). In addition, you can select how you want to be alerted when you have mail: by flashing icon, by alert box, or by sound. Use this tab to set your email program. Outlook Express is the default email program, but you can easily switch to another:

1. Choose Select from the Default Email pop-up menu.

2. In the resulting Finder Open dialog box, select another email program such as Netscape Communicator, Qualcomm's Eudora Pro or Eudora Lite, or whatever you want to use.

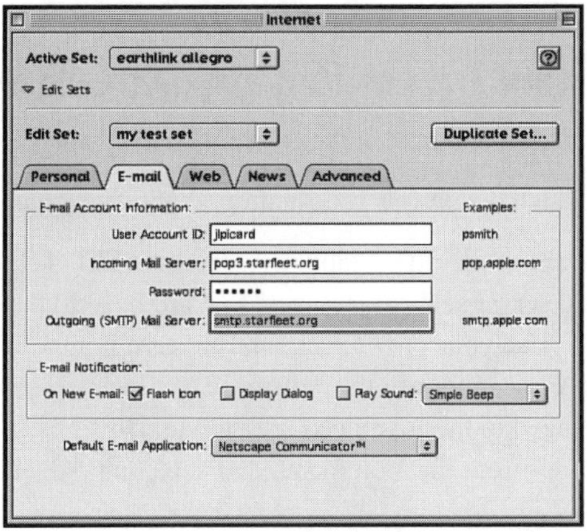

FIGURE **13.9**   The Email tab lets you select a default email program and lists your email user information as well as preferences.

USING THE WEB TAB

The Web tab lets you pick a home page and search page that automatically opens whenever you invoke your browser. This tab also is used to select a default browser and set up color options for types of links (active, selected, used, and default). Whichever browser you select has its own default home page that appears in the Home Page text box. If you do not like this page, copy an URL from a portal you do like and paste the data into the text box. For example, I don't like to use Netscape's Netcenter home page as my door to the Internet because it does not offer enough news. I changed my home page to http://my.excite.com.

> **Changing the Default Browser** Note that iMac dutifully assigns Microsoft Internet Explorer 4.01 as your default browser. Choose Select from the Default Web Browser pull-down menu on the Web screen to locate your copy of Netscape Navigator 4.0 or Communicator, if you want to use that browser. After you have located your alternative browser, it is easy to use the pull-down menu to switch browsers.

USING OTHER INTERNET CONFIGURATION TABS

There are two additional tabs on the Internet control panel:

- *News* This tab controls information about newsgroups.

- *Advanced Settings* This tab lets you adjust FTP, helper files, fonts, and server settings, subjects that are beyond the scope of this book. Use your browser manual to learn how to adjust these settings. You cannot use the Advanced Settings tab unless you have changed to the Advanced user mode. Do so by selecting User Modes from the Edit menu, and selecting Advanced.

GETTING READY FOR THE WEB

You are ready to get on the Web. But how do you dial your modem? How do you know you have connected correctly? How do you tell your iMac which browser to use after you are connected?

DIALING IN TO THE INTERNET

There are several ways to dial in to the Internet, including

- *The hard way*   Open the Remote Access control panel (shown in Figure 13.10) and click Connect.

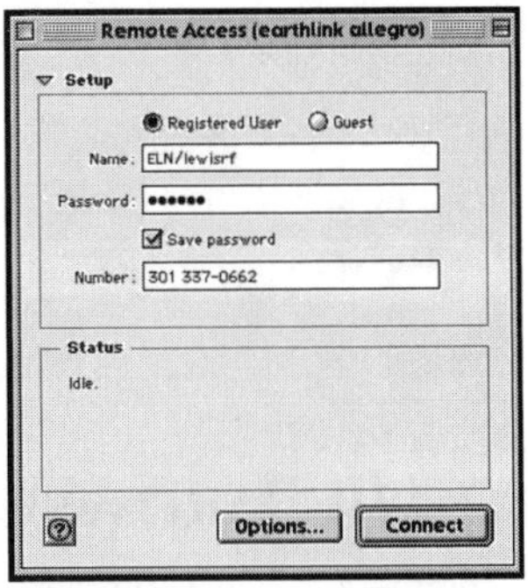

FIGURE 13.10   Use Remote Access to dial in to your Internet service provider.

- *The not-so-confusing way*   Click the Remote Access icon on your control strip and select Connect from the resulting menu.

- *The easy way*   Double-click the Browse the Internet icon on your desktop. When you double-click the icon you are automatically connected to your home page.

There is also the method you must use if you work for a company with an intranet, which is that you never have to dial in at all. Because you're connected to the Internet via a LAN, you're already dialed in.

NOW THAT YOU ARE IN...

If you successfully dial in to your Internet service provider (ISP), your browser displays the default URL—called the home page or the start page. After you're in, you can move around the World Wide Web. But how?

You can use an arcane addressing system called a *uniform resource locator* (URL) to reach the page you want to visit, or you can go to a page you previously identified as a Favorite (MSIE) or Bookmark (Navigator) by selecting that page from your Favorites/Bookmarks menu or toolbar button. You can also use various other buttons offered by your browser to get around. (See your browser manual for more details about navigating using your particular browser.)

What Are URLs Anyway? URL stands for *uniform resource locator*. URLs are the way that the Internet identifies accessible resources (Usenet newsgroup, file transfer servers, email, Web sites, chat rooms, and so forth). Every location on the Internet has its own unique URL.

WELCOME TO THE BROWSER WARS

Today, 90 percent of all Internet users use commercial browsers rather than homegrown varieties to surf the Web. Commercial browsers are improving on what they can interpret and display. Microsoft and Netscape are competing to create the ultimate browsing machine. Microsoft offers Internet Explorer, whereas Netscape provides Netscape Navigator.

INTERNET EXPLORER

Microsoft Internet Explorer 4.01 for the Macintosh (see Figure 13.11) is included on the iMac. This browser is entering its fourth iteration as a suite of tools to browse Web pages and online multimedia, email, chat, publish, and conference. And it is incorporating such new concepts as the capability to select the information that you want to view and have downloaded on a scheduled basis to your computer (this is called *push technology*).

You can download a free copy of the newest version of Microsoft's browser from `http://www.microsoft.com/ie/download/`. You can also order the update on a CD-ROM from that site.

FIGURE **13.11**   Microsoft Internet Explorer is a popular browser.

NETSCAPE NAVIGATOR

Netscape Navigator 4.0, shown in Figure 13.12, is included on the iMac
CD-ROM, but is not the default browser. The version included on the CD-
ROM is useful, but does not include Netscape Messenger (for email) as
well as a few other members of the Netscape suite. To download a free
copy of Netscape Navigator 4.06 (still lacking the features mentioned previously), visit http://www.netscape.com/download/index.html.
Alternatively, you can download Netscape Communicator free from this
site. Communicator is the full Netscape suite, complete with products for
browsing Web pages and multimedia content, emailing, chatting, publishing, and conferencing.

FIGURE **13.12**   Netscape Navigator is a fourth-generation browser package.

INTERNET SERVICES

Most people think of email when they think of Internet services, but email isn't the only way to communicate over the Internet; newsgroups and chat rooms are also quite popular. Not surprisingly, browsers are beefing up their feature sets to support filters, sorting, and embedded HTML in newsgroups, as well as virtual reality chat rooms with *avatars* (characters that represent you in these rooms).

EMAIL

There are currently two ways to transmit messages between computers using the Internet:

- General-purpose email packages that operate via ISPs. These packages include such products as Qualcomm's Eudora Lite and Eudora Pro, and Microsoft Outlook Express.

> **Changing Your Mail Program**   iMac uses Microsoft Outlook Express as its default email program, but also ships with Claris Emailer. You can change which mail program iMac uses by default by selecting a different program from the Email screen of the Internet control panel.

- Proprietary email systems built into commercial online services, such as CompuServe and America Online.

Recently, the larger search engines have begun offering free email services. The following engines offer free mailboxes on their systems along with providing you the capability to forward your mail from an assortment of email addresses to your free mailbox:

- Bigfoot   www.bigfoot.com
- Excite   www.excite.com
- Yahoo!   www.yahoo.com

> **Watch out!**   These Web-based email services are not secure. Information may be sent directly across the Internet without encryption unless the email service states that it uses secure sockets (SSL). Don't send anything you wouldn't want someone else to read!

> **iMac and Email**   Clicking the Mail icon on the iMac desktop opens your default email program and, if you are not online, dials your ISP via Remote Access. The email program (if set up to do so) sends and receives mail very rapidly without having to actually load an Internet browser or commercial service.

NEWSGROUPS

A *newsgroup* is a discussion group that's devoted to a particular topic. Every newsgroup is part of a hierarchy. The top level of the hierarchy consists of sites with names beginning in .sci, .talk, and .soc. Within these categories, you'll find groups covering almost every topic imaginable, organized into three basic areas:

- Alternative newsgroups (identified by .alt).

- Standard newsgroups (identified by .comp, .misc, .news, and .rec).

- Local newsgroups, which are set up for the benefit of a local community, organization, or university, and can have any name.

Table 14.1 presents general definitions of some of these groups.

TABLE 14.1   USENET PREFIX DEFINITIONS

PREFIX	DESCRIPTION
.alt	Alternative newsgroups that can be founded and managed by any Internet user.
.biz	An alternative newsgroup type dedicated to the discussion of business news, marketing, and advertising.
.comp	A standard newsgroup maintained by a Usenet site.
.misc	A standard newsgroup in which anything can be discussed that doesn't fit into other categories.
.news	A Usenet site.
.rec	A standard newsgroup where discussions center on hobbies and sports.
.sci	A standard newsgroup dealing with science topics.
.soc	A standard newsgroup dealing with social issues and socializing.
.talk	A standard newsgroup dealing with social issues.

Usenet newsgroups can handle only basic text. You can send graphics, sounds, and animation as *binaries* that must be decoded by the recipients' newsgroup reader software.

Each of the two main browser manufacturers provide newsgroup readers.

- Netscape Communicator's newsgroup reader is called *Collabra*.

- Microsoft Internet Explorer's reader, called *News*, can be accessed from Outlook Express.

Both of these news readers list Usenet newsgroups by their hierarchical names. You search for a group by its top-level prefix, and then burrow down within a category until you find the group you want. For example, to find alt.tv.highlander, you find the alt category, look for tv, and then hunt for highlander.

You can subscribe to groups that interest you. Subscribing to a group merely copies that group's name to your message center for easier access. Figure 13.13 shows the message center within Collabra. Note that it resembles Netscape Messenger's.

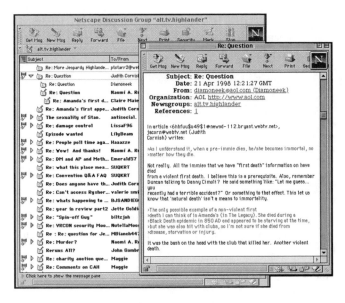

FIGURE 13.13   Netscape Collabra is one of many newsgroup reader applications that lets you manage the thousands of Usenet posts available for reading.

You'll want to exercise good *netiquette* if you want to avoid these two pernicious responses from obnoxious mailing list members:

- *Flaming*—Flaming is when another user (or users) sends you enormous quantities of email (sometimes hostile), with the intention of stuffing your mailbox.

- *Spamming*—Spamming is when an individual or organization sends you junk mail over the Internet, including offers of business opportunities, unwanted press releases, and worse.

To avoid these fates, follow these basic rules when visiting a newsgroup:

- Be a lurker—Just read along for a few days before jumping into a mailing list or Usenet group. Learn what topics are appropriate to query.

- Read the FAQs—A *FAQ* (short for *frequently asked questions*) is a series of basic questions and answers that gives you background information about a group. Reading FAQs puts you in the know. You can avoid repeating universal knowledge and asking silly questions.

- Don't type in capital letters—Typing in capitals is interpreted as shouting, and is very impolite. If you mean to emphasize a word, place asterisks around it.

- Keep your posts short—If you want to quote someone else's message within your message, don't copy the entire quote. Instead, copy only the snippets on which you want to comment.

CHAT ROOMS

Newsgroups present interactive communication on a delayed basis, whereas chat rooms provide interactive communication almost in real-time. I say almost because you still are typing furiously and sending your message to a group of people who then type furiously back for you to read line by line.

> ☼ **Want to Chat?** You need special software to use the
> Internet to chat. One of the most common Mac chat-
> ting tools is called *Global Chat*, a piece of shareware
> typically provided by your ISP.

There are two types of chats:

- *Static chats*, which resemble newsgroups in that you send a query out to the group and wait for someone to submit a response.

- *Classic chats*, which are fully interactive. Netscape Navigator, Internet Explorer, and AOL all offer Java-based chat engines that let you type messages in real-time.

SOME OF WHAT YOU'VE HEARD IS TRUE...

Although mostly safe, there are demons lurking on the Internet, as there are everywhere in society. They seem to show up most often in chat rooms and Usenet newsgroups. In chat rooms, everyone is anonymous and no one is who they seem to be. That means you can get caught in situations you would *never* get caught in if you were chatting face to face. Vile language, innuendo, smut, and stupidity run rampant. In addition, most of what you read is rumor and cannot be believed. Be cautious when using chat rooms and Usenets.

Do not:

- Give out your address or telephone number.

- Indicate where you live.

- Give out your email address.

Do:

- Avoid giving out your true identity.

- Stay away from chat rooms or Usenet newsgroups with subjects you feel uncomfortable about.

- Leave if you do not like what you are reading.

- Use a filter, such as SurfWatch (it comes with Internet Explorer), to screen out newsgroups and chat rooms you feel are inappropriate for children.

This lesson covers a lot of ground, from getting you connected to using the Internet to surf, chat, send email, and participate in newsgroups.

Lesson 14
File Sharing

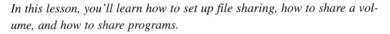

In this lesson, you'll learn how to set up file sharing, how to share a volume, and how to share programs.

As early as 1984, Macintosh computers enabled their users to communicate with other Macs and Apple printers were enabled to share data and programs without having to pass through an intermediary centralized file server. This capability is sometimes called *point-to-point* or *peer-to-peer* networking.

Apple Macs provide a perfect environment for this type of networking because networking protocols, software, and hardware (such as AppleTalk Filing Protocol, AppleShare software, and some sort of networking—in the iMac's case, Ethernet) is built in every Macintosh design. The AppleTalk protocols underlying this structure enable transparent communications between computers without the installation of additional devices or software. This is called *distributed file sharing*.

Running Ethernet with AppleTalk: iMac to Mac

The iMac does not come with the typical Macintosh network port (called *LocalTalk*), but instead comes equipped with an Ethernet port attached directly to its motherboard. You plug the 10BaseT thinnet connector or 100BaseT thicknet connector into the Ethernet port on the side of your iMac, and you are almost ready to network. If you are connecting the iMac to an existing Ethernet-based client/server network running file-serving operating systems such as AppleShare IP, NetWare, Windows NT, and so forth, you must have obtained a user ID and password from your network administrator to gain access to the server. When you have access permission, use the Chooser to select the server volume as discussed later in this chapter.

You can use AppleTalk to Ethernet bridge cables and software available from Farallon and other vendors to connect the iMac to other Macs via the Ethernet port (see Chapter 3, "Add-Ons: Extra Hardware," for a discussion of bridges). You do not need to run the iMac on a client/server network, but can use peer-to-peer networking to communicate between Macs. This type of networking uses built-in software called *File Sharing*. This chapter discusses the use of File Sharing with such a bridge network.

SETTING UP FILE SHARING

Mac 8.1 versus 8.5   All the screen shots in this chapter reference Mac OS 8.1 because that is the operating system version shipping on early iMacs. Be aware that the placement of some commands, namely Sharing Info, will change with Mac OS 8.5, but all the functions are identical between the two versions.

Setting up your Mac to share files is a multistep process:

1. Open the Users & Groups control panel, shown in Figure 14.1.

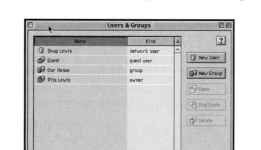

FIGURE **14.1**   The Users & Groups control panel is the first stop in creating your distributed network.

2. You will notice that you, the owner, already exist. Double-click the icon with your name to see your password and computer's name (see Figure 14.2). If the information is missing, type it in.

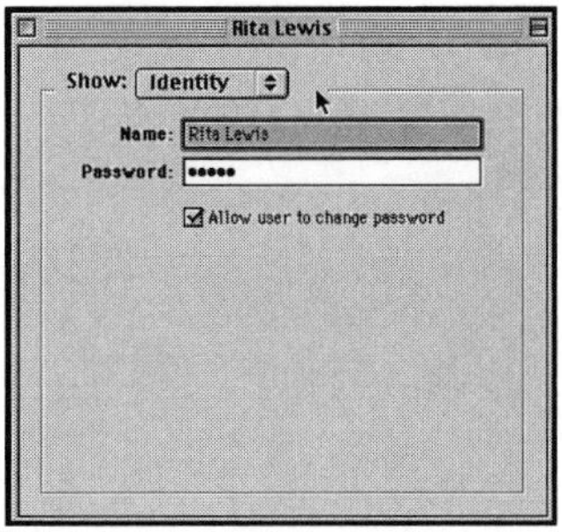

FIGURE **14.2**   Use the User dialog box to identify yourself to the network.

3. Use the pop-up menu to shift to the Sharing screen, where you assign permissions as to who can share your computer. This is called *assigning groups* (*groups* contain those users who are permitted to share folders and files with each other).

4. Open the File Sharing control panel (see Figure 14.3). Your name, your computer's name, and your password should already be entered. If these items are missing, go ahead and type them in.

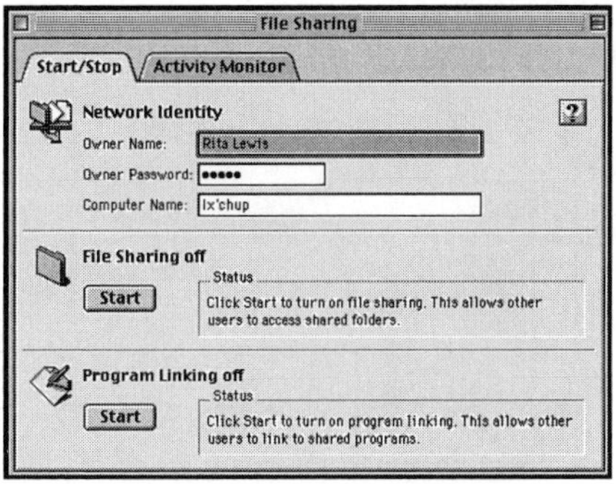

FIGURE **14.3**   The File Sharing control panel turns File Sharing on and off.

5. Click Start to turn on File Sharing.

> **Turning AppleTalk On**   AppleTalk needs to be on
> before you can turn on file sharing. Select AppleTalk
> from the Control Panel pop-up menu on the Apple
> menu. If AppleTalk is off, you will receive an alert box
> asking if you want to turn it on. Click Yes. You can
> also turn on AppleTalk in the Chooser.

Next, select the folders and hard disks that you will allow to be shared on
the network. Only you can designate how your files will be accessed and
by whom. The Sharing command on the desktop File menu is the tool
used to designate access privileges for your files and folders.

1. Place the files you want to share with other users into a folder.

2. Select the folder containing the files you want to share.

3. Click the Sharing command on the desktop's File menu.

4. A window with the same name as the folder or disk you want to
   share opens, as shown in Figure 14.4. The top of the window
   describes the location of the sharable folder or disk.

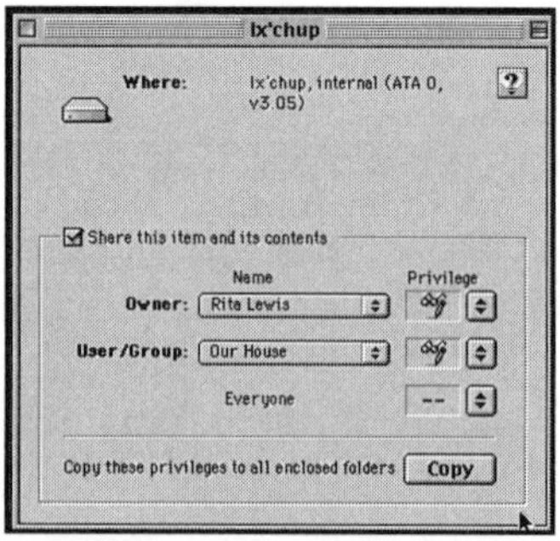

FIGURE 14.4   Select a folder and choose Sharing from the File menu
to permit sharing.

Make an Alias   Creating an alias for the documents you want to share protects the original file from being destroyed by someone using your disk. Create an alias by selecting the file and choosing Make Alias from the File menu (or press ⌘+M). The person using your disk can make changes to the alias copy of the file that are reflected by the original, but can remove only the alias (not the original).

Share at the Root Level   A folder or disk cannot be shared if it contains a folder that is already designated as shared. If you place your shared folder at the highest level of your folder hierarchy, called the *root*, you avoid having the system give you a message that the folder you want to access to is not accessible because there is a shared folder inside of it.

SHARING A VOLUME

File Sharing is transparent after you set up the network. To access a shared file, do the following:

1. Select Chooser from the Apple menu.

2. In the Chooser, shown in Figure 14.5, select the AppleShare driver icon from the Printer Driver area, and highlight the file server you want to access from the list of file servers. (If necessary, select the network zone where the file resides.)

Using Volumes   Volumes selected in the Chooser are displayed on your Mac as hard disks, and can be opened and used in the same way that you use your own local disks.

FIGURE 14.5   The Chooser is a multipurpose utility for selecting network and printer drivers, as well as zones.

3. Click the OK button.

4. If you have been given a password and registered name by the owner of the Macintosh you want to access, click the Registered User radio button when the system requests your AppleShare user status (see Figure 14.6). Enter your registered username and password in the spaces provided, and click OK.

> **Using Guest Privileges**   If you are not a registered user, click the Guest radio button (if there are no guest privileges for the file, the button is dimmed).

> **Registered Names and Passwords**   Before you can access another person's shared items as a registered user, you must know your registered name and password on the other person's system. If the network is large, you might also need to know the zone where the other Macintosh is located.

5. The system displays a list of sharable files you can access, as shown in Figure 14.7. Select the file or files you want to access and click OK.

FIGURE **14.6**   File Sharing has built-in security, requesting your user ID and password before it lets you access folders on another Mac.

> **Unavailable Files**   Any files that are not currently available or are already accessed by you appear dimmed.

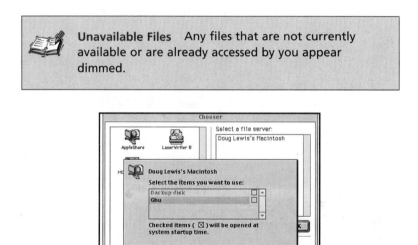

FIGURE **14.7**   Folders you have been given permission to share are listed in this dialog box. Select a folder to mount it on your Mac.

6. An icon depicting the shared folder, called a *volume*, appears on your Macintosh in the right-hand side of the screen and acts like a hard disk (see Figure 14.8).

To terminate File Sharing, simply throw the shared file or volume into your Trash Can.

FIGURE **14.8**   The shared volume is displayed on your desktop. Its networked icon indicates that it is a shared disk.

AppleTalk Access   AppleTalk must be active for you to link to another Macintosh on the network. Click the radio button labeled Active in the Chooser if it is not on.

What the Owner Sees   When someone throws away a shared file, the Macintosh owner receives a folder on the desktop labeled Network Trash folder. As long as the user does not empty the Trash Can, the owner can restore the item by dragging it out of the Trash folder and renaming it. Owners can prevent the trashing of shared folders by changing the access privileges for their shared files.

SHARING PROGRAMS

If your organization has applications such as databases, spreadsheets, or desktop-publishing programs that are licensed for group use, File Sharing enables you to access this software from your Mac using the Program Linking tool. After you enable the use of this tool by clicking the Program Linking button in the File Sharing control panel, you'll be allowed to select networked programs from the Chooser.

If you have a program on your machine that you would like to share on your network, do the following:

1. Select Sharing from the File menu.

2. When the Sharing dialog box appears, click the Allow Remote Program Linking box.

Local Program Sharing   You do not have to use the Sharing command to link to other programs on your own Macintosh. Use it only if you want to link with a remote program.

Dimmed Sharing Command   If you have not enabled sharing via the File Sharing control panel, the Sharing command is dimmed in the menu. It is also dimmed if you have not preselected a program before highlighting the command or if the program does not support program linking.

Sharing Command Window   The Sharing command activates a window with the same name as the program you want to share. The top of the window describes the location of the sharable folder.

PERFORMANCE ISSUES WITH FILE SHARING

You can minimize the tendency of shared Macs to have degraded performance by doing the following:

- Assign an alias to a shared volume you have accessed from another Mac. Next time you want to use it, double-click the alias to bring its volume onto your system.

- Limit the number of folders you allow to be shared by placing all the files you are sharing into a single folder and designating that folder as the shared item.

- Limit the number of people who access your Mac. Make it a rule that work is performed on the local Mac and not on remote nodes.

- Share as few files as possible. This is a good security procedure, because fewer available files means less possible damage.

- Limit the security levels. Keep it simple so that managing and untangling a confusion of passwords and access permissions does not take up all your time.

- Use the same registered names on all Macs on the network to avoid confusion.

- Avoid launching an application on a volume you are sharing; the performance of both Macs becomes too slow to do anything else on these computers. For best performance, you should copy a file to your local disk, edit it and copy it back to the other, file-shared disk.

In this lesson, you learned how to set up File Sharing, how to share a volume, and how to share programs. You also learned about some of the performance issues associated with File Sharing.

LESSON 15
PERSONAL WEB SERVING

In this lesson you will learn the ins and outs of personal Web serving, including setting up Web Sharing, turning on Web Sharing, and accessing the server. CGI scripts will also be discussed.

The Personal Web Sharing feature allows your iMac to become a server, enabling you to electronically publish materials including

- Bulletin boards
- Chat rooms
- Forms
- Web pages

Because it is assumed that you will be serving a limited number of people who have access to your domain address, your iMac can handle the load.

Internet Server Solution When you find that you are getting too many hits, try Apple's Internet Server Solution for the World Wide Web package to create the dedicated server you need.

PERSONAL WEB SHARING

Think of Web Sharing as File Sharing over the Internet. Web Sharing is a distributed server that lets others on your intranet access and send you documents over the intranet. Any file placed in your Web Pages folder can be served using the Personal Web Sharing server. You simply place HTML documents, CGIs, Java applets, and so forth in your Web Pages folder, and your server processes these files and serves the results to those users who access your address. This means that anyone with a browser, whether it is Netscape Navigator or Communicator or Microsoft Internet Explorer on a PC or a Mac, can read what has been published, and then respond interactively (if the proper software resides in the Web Pages folder).

SETTING UP WEB SHARING

This section assumes that you already have access to the corporate intranet or to the Internet.

After you have logged on to the Internet or your corporate intranet, set up Personal Web Sharing as follows:

1. Open the Personal Web Sharing control panel from the Control Panels hierarchical menu on the Apple menu.

2. In the Personal Web Sharing control panel (see Figure 15.1), click the Select button next to Web Folder to indicate where on your hard disk you are storing the folders and files you want to share over the Internet.

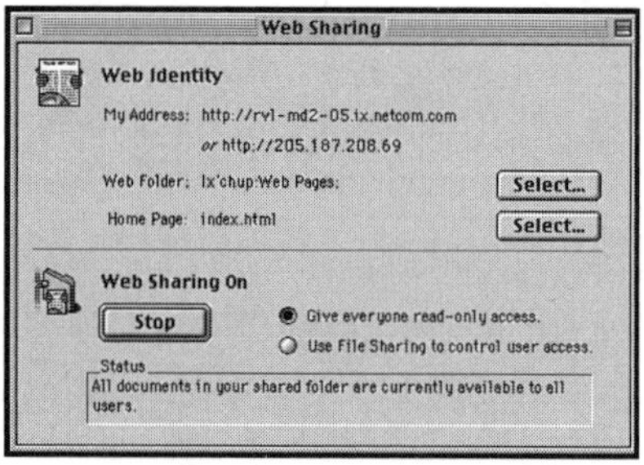

FIGURE 15.1 Click the appropriate Select button to assign a sharing folder and default start page.

3. Select a folder from the Finder list box.

4. Click the Select button next to Home Page to indicate which file is your default or starting page (typically named index.html).

5. Select a file from the resulting Finder list box.

FIGURE 15.2   Select the page you want to use as your default starting page.

The default page will be the first page that users see every time they log
on to your site.

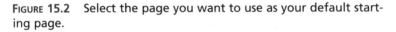

Adobe SiteMill   Remember that links stay linked only
if you do not move documents out of their subfolders.
Use Adobe SiteMill to ensure that all your links work
before you turn on the Web server.

The Personal Web Sharing server can be secured so that only certain people can access its contents. Web Sharing works with the Sharing command
from OS 8 File Sharing to set up access privileges in the same fashion as
they worked for File Sharing. See Chapter 14, "File Sharing," for a discussion of setting permissions.

TURNING ON WEB SHARING

To turn on Web Sharing, do the following:

1. Select the Web Sharing control panel from the Control Panels
   pop-up menu on the Apple menu.

2. In the resulting Web Sharing dialog box, click Start.

3. The server checks whether an IP address has been assigned, and
   if not, it calls the intranet or Internet service provider (ISP) to
   establish one.

Notice that the Web Address space contains two addresses:

- The first address is the domain name for your server.
- The second address is the actual IP address of your server.

Users can reach your default Web page using either the domain name or the IP address. Alternatively, you can pay $100 to InterNIC to purchase an actual domain name, such as www.*yourcompany*.com, which you can then lease for $50 per year.

 What's My Address? If you forget the address, open the Web Sharing control panel. The address is displayed whenever the server is active.

 Copying the Address You can copy the IP address to your Clipboard for pasting into documents or emails by selecting Copy Address from the File menu when the Web Sharing control panel is open.

You can control how many people can access your server (hence, you can control its performance) by limiting or increasing the amount of memory allocated to the server. Do the following:

1. Select the Web Sharing entry in the Extensions folder of your System folder.

2. Open the Get Info dialog box (press ⌘+I) to increase the preferred memory size. (Make sure that your server is turned off before increasing or decreasing its memory.)

3. Turn the server back on to effect changes to its performance parameters.

ACCESSING THE SERVER

Anyone with a browser can type your server's IP address and gain access to either your default home page or the Personal NetFinder. I have placed my own Web site in the Web Pages folder that resides on my Mac. When the Web Sharing server is on, that is what people are able to view and use.

 Create Your Own Web Pages   Use an HTML editor such as PageMill or Claris HomePage to create your own pages.

Figure 15.3 shows that what resides in the Web Pages folder becomes the contents of the server. Drag and drop files into the folder to change the contents of the server.

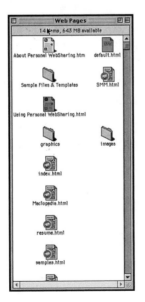

FIGURE 15.3   Any file placed in your Web Sharing folder is available for browsing over the Internet.

Creating Your Own FTP Server   Your Web server can
be a document repository and not an electronic publishing house when you set the home page identifier
to None and use the Personal NetFinder (see Figure
15.4). When you select None, Personal NetFinder
shows a list view of the contents of the Web Pages
folder on your surfer's browsers. Users can then
choose which document to view by clicking it, as you
would in the Finder's List view. Such a listing is useful
if you are using the Web Sharing server to upload and
download files (such as an FTP server).

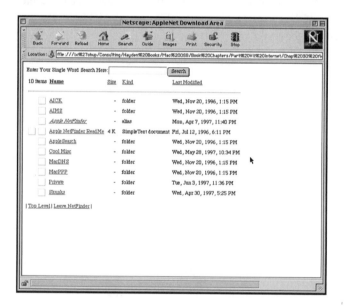

FIGURE **15.4**   Your Mac can become a personal FTP server with
Personal NetFinder.

CGI SCRIPTS

A *CGI* (short for *common gateway interface*) is not a programming language; rather, it is a set of conventions or rules for setting up two-way communications between the server's computer and the browser's computer. CGIs, which have been written for every computer platform and can be written in almost any computer language, provide the roadmap for the way that Web clients and servers handle requests for executing and sending out the results of programs processed on the server.

CGIs can be used to create the following features for your Web pages (this list is by no means exhaustive):

- *Forms and guest books*   Most CGIs process information via Web page forms because forms offer a flexible way of getting information from people who visit your site and returning information back to them. Specialized forms called *guest books* collect information about visitors; other forms take information and return data to your readers; still other forms offer ways to email or fax information.

- *Counters*   Not long ago it became incredibly popular to have a counter on your Web site's home page. There's no point to this other than to let people know how popular your site is (or to show off your Web know-how).

- *Active images*   Active images are graphics with *hot spots* that can be clicked to access their underlying hypertext link. There are two types of active images, depending on where the information used to create the link resides: server-side and client-side. However, for those server-side active images to work, you need to have a CGI on the server that can process the information that comes in when the mouse is clicked.

- *Animations*   Animated GIFs can be created just like cartoons used to be: by drawing a sequence of pictures, each one slightly different, and displaying them rapidly one after another. There are three ways to receive moving pictures on your Web page:

    - *Client-pull animations*   Client-pull refers to the fact that the browser requests an object from the server (meaning that the animation is initiated by the browser).

- *Server-push animations*   The benefit of server-push animation is that it is triggered on the server-side by a CGI, and so it is capable of affecting individual elements on your page.

- *Animated GIFs*   Netscape Navigator uses a feature of GIFs called *GIF animation* that incorporates all the animation frames into one file that downloads as a piece. This is a more efficient use of the server and saves storage space as well.

- *Online stores*   If you are creating your Web site to sell items, you can use a standalone CGI program serving as a product catalog. Another CGI is used to process the orders. In addition, you can generate dynamic catalog pages and take electronic orders.

- *Database processing*   When you collect information, such as the stuff you got from your forms and CGI scripts, you need to put it somewhere. That somewhere is called a *database*. Database CGIs place the information from a browser's form in a semi-permanent repository. The CGI can then retrieve parts of the information, based on options selected by the user, and redisplay them on a page.

To learn more about CGI scripting, check out the following sites:

- http://hoohoo.ncsa.uiuc.edu/cgi/intro.html

- http://www.yahoo.com/Computers_and_Internet/Internet/World_Wide_Web/CGI_Common_Gateway_Interface/

- http://www.comvista.com/net/www/cgi.html

- http://www.eff.org/~erict/Scripts

- http://www.worldwidemart.com/Scripts/

This lesson explains the ins and outs of personal Web serving, including setting up Web Sharing, turning on Web Sharing, and accessing the server. CGI scripts are also discussed.

Lesson 16

Talking to the Other Guys

In this lesson you will learn how to share data between files, between programs, and over the Internet.

So, you've created the ultimate report containing beautiful typeset text, sophisticated illustrations, and a brilliant analysis on spreadsheets, and you want to share it electronically with the world (or your workgroup). iMac has three information-sharing problems that immediately hit you in the face:

- How can you provide another person—who might not even have a Mac (for shame!)—the capability to open and view your document on their computer?

- If your co-worker can't open the document, how can you share the information contained within the document?

- If you can open and view a document on another person's computer, how do you ensure that all your formatting, including typography, is visible?

Don't fret. iMac provides a series of tools that make it relatively easy to share documents—or their contents—with those other users, whether they use a Mac or not.

Sharing Data Versus Sharing Documents

One of the ways that the Macintosh is different from the Intel world is in the imposition of standards on software that runs on the operating system. On the Mac, you could traditionally take data from one program and use it in another because all the software recognized basic features of Mac files. You might not realize it, but on a PC, individual software hasn't a clue or a care about which file goes with which program. Windows 95 has gotten smarter about this, but underneath the surface, even Windows 95 is still DOS.

WHAT ARE FILE FORMATS?

The goal in computing is to produce information that can be used and shared. This sounds simple enough, except for one small problem: Software that does this work on computers handles the task of telling the screen and printer how to display and manipulate text and graphics in many different ways.

The codes used to display and print information in a document compose the file format. The *file format* tells the program how information (text, graphics, and formatting) is stored. The trouble is that one program's file format might not be legible to another program. Thus, you might not be able to view the information in a document if you don't have the program installed on the computer that produced the document. If the program you are importing the document into does not contain the same feature set as the document's originator, you will lose the formatting based on the missing features. Sometimes trying to open a foreign file might crash the importing program. You must be aware of file formats when importing and exporting files.

There are many file formats; the ones that concern you the most are those used to share information between software packages, called *file interchange formats*. The granddaddy of all interchange formats is called *ASCII* (pronounced as-key), an acronym for *American Standard Code for Information Interchange*. Macintosh understands an extended version of ASCII containing 256 characters (those Option-key characters such as ™, ®, ©, and foreign language markings are added to the standard 128 characters).

ASCII assigns a unique number to every letter, number, and symbol; these numbers are understood by most software programs. The program takes the ASCII codes and matches them to corresponding characters. ASCII is the underlying character code that most programs build on to handle text, although ASCII is *raw* text without formatting.

> **Moving Text Between Programs** You can always move ASCII (called text on the iMac) between software programs, although you will lose any bold, italics, tab stops, hanging indentations, and so forth in the conversion process.

There are several file interchange formats that capture more formatting than simple ASCII. The problem is that with more formatting comes additional danger that the importing program does not support the format feature and you lose your data. Not all formats are supported by all programs. Try each flavor to find the one that transfers the most information to the new program. They are as follows:

- *Document content architecture (DCA)*—This is a PC-based file format that can be translated by MacLink Plus/PC and MacLink/Translators. When using this format you lose fonts, styles, and size information.

- *Rich text format (RTF)*—This is the strongest interchange format, retaining a lot of information about font, styles, and sizes across programs. Not all Mac word processors support RTF, although it is useful to use RTF if you are moving PageMaker or QuarkXPress files across platforms between Windows and Mac.

- *Data interchange format (DIF)*—This is another PC-based file format that assists in the transfer of spreadsheet and database information. Cell formatting and width information are lost in the translation. MacLink Plus/PC and MacLink/Translators support DIF.

- *Symbolic link (SYLK)*—This file format translates spreadsheet and database information while retaining some formatting, including commas, column width, and cell alignments. Font, style, and size information is lost in the transfer.

- *Encapsulated PostScript (EPS)*—This file format converts PostScript-based graphics and special effects from native formats to one that most PC programs can accept. Only PostScript devices (such as PostScript Level 2 laser printers) can understand and print EPS graphics.

- *Tagged-image file format (TIFF)*—A file format that transfers bitmapped graphics between computer platforms. TIFF is supported by many PC and Mac scanners and is independent of specific computer or graphic resolutions. The files are very large and cumbersome to store and load.

- *PICT format*—This is the basic Mac graphics file format encoded into the Mac's screen description language, QuickDraw. You can combine bitmapped with object-oriented graphic images into a single PICT file. There is minimal PC program support for PICT, although MacLink Plus/PC and MacLink/Translators do provide translators for PICT to Windows Metafile format.

Many popular software applications provide file format translators that go beyond ASCII to translate the special codes used to indicate formatting from one file format to another. Thus, WordPerfect, Microsoft Word, and Nisus NisusWriter translate documents from native formats to another program's format—but not all programs are as accommodating.

You set the file format in the Save As dialog box (opened by selecting Save As on the File menu of almost every Macintosh program). Use the File Format pop-up menu (see Figure 16.1) to select a file interchange format for your document. The formats listed are those supported by the program you are using. Each program supports a different range of formats, from Word's extensive list to Freehands' very short list (Freehand, PICT, and EPS).

SHARING DATA BETWEEN FILES

There are two tried-and-true methods of copying information between files on the Mac:

- You can copy and paste information via the Clipboard.

- You can drag and drop the information between files.

Dragging and dropping is neat. Select the item you want to copy and, while holding down the mouse, move the cursor to where you want to copy the information to. When you release the mouse, the selected material is copied to the new location.

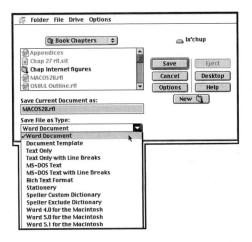

FIGURE **16.1** Use the Save As dialog box to select a file interchange format for your document.

Use drag and drop to copy items between files or to copy graphics from files to the desktop for use as backgrounds on Web pages or as wallpaper on the desktop screen of the Appearance control panel. This latter method creates a Picture Clippings File (see Figure 16.2). (Be sure to save the new clippings file in the Desktop Pictures folder in the Appearance folder in the System Folder).

FIGURE **16.2** Click and drag an item from the Scrapbook or another file to the desktop to create a Picture Clippings File.

You can also select text and drag it to the desktop. You can then use the text repeatedly by dragging its Clippings file from the desktop to an open document in any program that supports drag and drop. This is handy for inserting your address, telephone numbers, URLs, email addresses, and other information into multiple places.

SHARING FILES BETWEEN PROGRAMS

It is one thing to share files between Macintosh programs, and it is another related and more challenging thing to share Macintosh files with Windows programs and vice versa. File Sharing on a Mac is relatively straightforward because of the advent of *Easy Open*. (Note that Easy Open has been supplanted in Mac OS 8.5 by a better control panel called *File Exchange* that works in a similar fashion).

USING FILE EXCHANGE FOR TRANSLATION

The File Exchange control panel's File Translation screen (see Figure 16.3) maps orphan files with compatible applications so that they can be opened and read. Double-clicking any file, whether it has a creator identified or not, will launch an application that can read that file. If File Exchange cannot identify the creator of a file, it displays a dialog box asking you to select the most likely candidate.

File Exchange's File Translation tool gets a strong helping hand from a third-party application that is resident on the iMac called MacLink Plus/Translators from DataViz. MacLink Plus contains a vast array of formatting filters that convert file formats from one format to another, including Internet formats such as HTML, GIF, and JPEG. MacLink Plus works with Easy Open to convert orphaned files to legible files by linking appropriate converters to applications.

Macs and PCs are not the same species. These two computer systems cannot readily communicate because the ways that information is stored and processed (disk and file formats) are so different. Reading PC files on a Mac used to be impossible. Thankfully, Apple developed two tools that it includes with iMac that make exchanging files with PCs much easier: PC Exchange and Easy Open. Mac OS 8.5 (and iMac) further simplifies file conversion by combining these two tools into one single control panel called File Exchange. I have already discussed the File Translation screen portion of File Exchange, but you can also use File Exchange's PC Exchange screen to automatically translate PC file formats to Mac file formats on-the-fly.

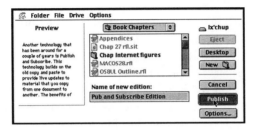

FIGURE 16.3   The File Translation screen lets you manually or automatically map orphan files to compatible applications.

USING THE PC EXCHANGE SCREEN

In this day and age of mixed platform offices, it is sad but true that you will run into people who do not use Macs. Sometimes these PC users might have information they want to share with you. How can you get a PC file recognized by your Mac so that the appropriate program can read the file? The PC Exchange portion of File Exchange performs several hidden jobs:

- It allows the reading of PC disks on Macs.

- It allows you to open PC files in their corresponding Mac programs.

PC Exchange works invisibly to display PC files on your Mac. But PC Exchange goes further than simply allowing you to see files on the screen. PC Exchange is a control panel that lets you map file extensions between PCs and Macs. Extension mapping lets you create a relationship between the Mac's types and creators with a PC file's extensions (the three-letter suffix) in most PC filenames. You can then open PC files by double-clicking them as you would a Mac file.

The PC Exchange screen of the File Exchange control panel provides the capability to pick a program to associate with an extension, and then further link the creator and type by looking at all the options on a hierarchical menu. This is handy because a PC extension such as .TIF can be read by many Mac programs, such as ClarisWorks, MacDraw Pro, Color It, Macromedia Freehand, Adobe PageMaker, and so forth. You can also set up proper MIME types for transmission of files over the Internet between Macs and PCs.

PC Exchange adds another function to Macs: the capability to mount PC-formatted removable disks such as Iomega Zip or Jaz drives, Syquest EZ135s, or Bernoulli cartridges on the Mac desktop. With this option selected, you can slip PC-formatted removables in your appropriate disk drives and they properly appear on your desktop. (Remember that the iMac uses USB ports. PC Exchange works with removables connected using USB or bridges to translate alien files to iMac formats.)

Watch the Filename Lengths! Windows 95 lets you give filenames of up to 256 characters, but Macs can only handle 31 characters, and worse still, PC Exchange works with the older Windows 3.1 rules of an eight-character limit on filenames. Thus, when files are copied to and from PC disks, filenames are truncated to eight characters and a three-character suffix.

One solution is to give your files eight-character names if they are going to be read by Macs and PCs, or get a more robust conversion program such as Software Architect's DOS Mounter 95 that supports Windows 95 file-naming conventions and still limits your filenames to the 31 characters that the Mac can recognize as a name. Always try to add the suffix to Mac files that are bound for PCs, even though these suffixes have no meaning on Macs, because they are crucial to safe computing on the PC side.

SHARING FILES OVER A NETWORK AND THE INTERNET

When you want to exchange files over a network to PCs or between your Mac and an online service, you want to retain the information stored in the data and resource forks. The most secure way of making sure that you can reconstruct your Mac files or applications after they are downloaded is to convert your Mac files to MacBinary format prior to sending them.

MacBinary is a special file format for telecommunications that strips the information off the data and resource forks and creates a special header containing this data along with the file's Finder attributes that it installs at the beginning of the file. Most telecommunications programs and FTP programs let you specify that you want to transmit the Mac files in MacBinary. Note that programs such as Fetch rename your files with a .bin suffix to indicate they are MacBinary files. You can also manually translate your files to MacBinary format using Aladdin Software's StuffIt Deluxe.

When you download files to your Mac, software such as Aladdin Software's StuffIt Expander, which comes with Mac OS 8's Internet Access package, converts the file back to a standard Mac file format. You will know that a file is in MacBinary format because it is labeled with a .bin suffix.

You might also see .hqx or .uu as suffixes. These are two other communications file formats used to transmit Mac or PC files. The BinHex format (.hqx) is used to convert Mac files to reside safely on UNIX servers (such as those used on the Internet). The UUcode format (.uu) is used to convert files for use on PCs. You can set up StuffIt Expander to automatically decode these formats as well (see Figure 16.4). Double-click the StuffIt Expander icon on your desktop and select Preferences from the File menu. Select the options you want to automatically invoke when you drop items on to the icon (or download files using the Netscape Navigator browser).

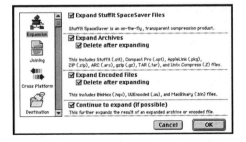

FIGURE 16.4   Set up StuffIt Expander to automatically decode communication file formats such as BinHex, uucode, or MacBinary.

Note that the DropStuff application that also comes with the Internet Access software in Mac OS8 converts files to BinHex format during the stuffing process if so set in its Preferences dialog box (located on the File menu). Then, whenever you drag and drop a folder or file onto the DropStuff alias icon residing on your desktop, its contents are encoded and stuffed automatically.

The Mac is smart, but Wintel machines are not so smart because they must deal with more variety. If you download a Mac file to a PC, it does not have the software to convert and decompress MacBinary files. Use Sneaker Net to carry the file from the PC back to a Mac and decode and decompress the file using StuffIt Expander. You can also retransmit the file from the PC to your Mac and have it automatically decoded as it downloads. It is possible that the Wintel machine you are communicating with has Aladdin's Stuffit Expander for Windows installed. If Stuffit for Windows is available, it will decode MacBinary and unstuff a .sit file on the Windows side.

SHARING DOCUMENTS ONLINE

One of the most frustrating things about exchanging documents is how messed up fonts, typographical formatting, and layout can get if the person you are exchanging a file with does not have the same program or fonts installed as you. Before documents could be published on CD-ROMs, intranets, or other online document distribution systems, this problem had to be resolved.

We are not at the paperless office yet, but we are getting close. Many vendors have searched for a method to embed fonts and formatting in a document and still keep the size of the document manageable for transmitting. Several solutions to this problem have been proposed, and the winner at this time seems to be Adobe Systems' Acrobat.

PORTABLE DOCUMENT FORMAT (PDF)

All electronic publishing tools operate by "printing" a document to a special file. Some programs require you to select a driver in the Chooser prior to printing. Acrobat's Distiller operates through a command on the File menu of Acrobat-savvy programs (such as Adobe PageMill) to create a portable document format (PDF) file.

Adobe designed this PDF format to be PostScript-based, thus preserving the format and layout of text and graphics as if they had been printed on a PostScript laser printer. The PDF does not contain embedded fonts, but rather the PostScript-based descriptions of how to build the fonts (their height, width, weight, names, and styles, and so forth). Acrobat uses several substitution fonts and a technology called Multiple Masters to build missing fonts on-the-fly. Because the actual fonts are not resident in the files, and the files are compressed, Acrobat files are very small and easy to transmit online.

You need to have Adobe Distiller installed to create a PDF. Distiller is part of a suite of five programs that together constitute Adobe Acrobat Pro 3.0. You view Acrobat files using the Acrobat Reader that is freely distributed by Adobe all over the Internet (check out http://www.adobe.com) and is included in the Internet Access component of Mac OS 8.5. Acrobat also includes collaboration software, Acrobat for Workgroups; Acrobat Search, a powerful indexing tool to create searchable documents; Acrobat Catalog; and Acrobat Capture, an optical character recognition package that lets you scan items and automatically convert them to PDFs for distribution. With the Acrobat Reader and Adobe Type Manager (ATM) installed, you can read PDFs containing text, animated graphics, movies, and sounds (see Figure 16.5).

Acrobat Distiller provides the capability to convert documents to PDFs in background. Set up a Watcher folder and place any documents you want to convert in the folder and Distiller converts them while you are working on something else.

Adobe Acrobat Pro is expensive ($450), and is a memory and storage hog. Other companies have created less popular, but more efficient, portable document converters. These are discussed in the next section.

COMMON GROUND, ENVOY, AND REPLICA

Adobe is not the only vendor to create electronic publishing tools. Common Ground Software (formerly No Hands Software) provides Common Ground for considerably less than Adobe's Acrobat. Common Ground costs around $100 and can create Digital Paper versions of documents that can be viewed using the Common Ground viewer. Like PDFs, DPs can be annotated, searched, and indexed. You can add hypertext links and PostScript graphics to Digital Paper files. The benefit of Common Ground is that you can embed its very efficient MiniViewer in your Digital Paper file so that the recipient does not need to have access to a viewer to be able to read your document.

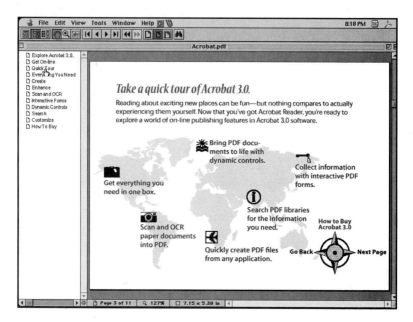

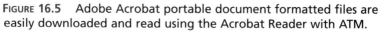

FIGURE 16.5   Adobe Acrobat portable document formatted files are easily downloaded and read using the Acrobat Reader with ATM.

Corel inherited Envoy from Novell when it bought WordPerfect. Envoy is another electronic document tool that lets you create portable documents from WordPerfect files.

Farallon offers Replica, another electronic publishing tool. Common Ground, Envoy, and Replica have not had the success of Acrobat. The more Acrobat becomes ubiquitous on the Net, the more of a de facto standard it becomes, driving these other products out of the market.

In this lesson you learned how to share data between files, between programs, and over the Internet.

LESSON 17

TROUBLE-
SHOOTING THE
iMAC

In this lesson you will learn to troubleshoot your system and resolve various types of problems, including hardware and software problems.

When you feel sick and can't put your finger on why, you call the doctor, who examines your symptoms and comes up with a diagnosis. Troubleshooting an iMac works the same way:

1. A problem happens, crashing your computer.

2. You identify the problem by running a diagnostic software suite or by manually checking out the possible causes.

3. You or the assisting software come up with a definition of the problem and a possible solution.

4. You try to implement the cure, let a specialist (the iMac technician) fix the machine, or buy a new iMac.

What exactly is meant by *crash*? Several things:

- Your iMac's cursor freezes and moving the mouse produces no cursor movement.

- The Finder displays an alert with a bomb and a very cryptic error message, and may or may not let you restart, depending on the severity of the problem.

- A blank alert box appears and the iMac freezes.

- You get a low memory alert and a few seconds later your program dies. You are returned to the desktop, and then the Finder bombs.

The good news is that iMacs seldom crash without something you added being the cause, be it a system extension that conflicts with others, a non-compliant application (one that doesn't follow Apple's Human Interface

Guidelines), or a peripheral device that is not installed correctly—all problems that can be researched and solved.

The bad news is that when the iMac crashes, it crashes. So preventive medicine (backups, frequent defragmenting, and frequent checkups) should be performed so that crashes don't happen, and if they do you don't lose much of your work.

PREVENTIVE MEDICINE: COLLECTING A SOFTWARE TOOLKIT

Here's some good news: Intel PCs crash a lot. That means software vendors have seen a business opportunity and developed software to battle errors. iMac users have benefited from the experience and expertise of these vendors, such as Symantec, Qualcomm, MicroMat, and FWB, as well as other utility players such as AlSoft and MacAfee. Several good diagnostic tools are on the market to assist you in your identification task. It is a good idea, even if you are apprehensive about getting into the guts of your iMac, to purchase diagnostic software to have on hand if and when something bad happens. Here are some tools that I strongly recommend you get:

- *Backup software*—There are currently three ways to maintain a backup copy of the contents of your hard drive(s): manually, via a local backup program, or via a remote Internet-based backup system.

> **When Not to Back Up Manually**   Don't manually perform a backup unless you have a very small hard drive or few important files; the volume of files is too great. Use a backup system such as Dantz Retrospect (locally) or Netscape's Atreiva (remotely).

- *Diagnostic and repair software*—You need an automated helper to delve into the internals of your hard drive, system files, and ROM to hunt down errors. There are two powerhouse programs on the market to perform this work:

- *Symantec Norton Utilities Version 5.0*—Norton Utilities provides a plethora of tools that you can use to perform disk maintenance (such as optimization and defragmentation) as well as to recover from a variety of software and hardware problems. It provides tools that enable you to recover your files in the event of an accidental deletion, helps you protect your system when one of your applications crashes, and enables you to rate your machine's performance so that you can see whether problems are degrading your Mac's performance.

- *MicroMat's TechTools 2.0*—If you have upgraded your drives to HFS+, upgrade to TechTools 2.0. TechTools provides two levels of diagnosis: basic and advanced. Although it lacks the plethora of tools provided by Norton Utilities, it checks your iMac and its peripherals much more deeply and thoroughly than Norton.

- *System Extension management software*—An important piece of preventive medicine is the management of your startup files and system extensions. Apple provides the Extension Manager in Mac OS 8, but this program is unwieldy and limited in scope. Instead of using Extension Manager, consider purchasing Casady & Greene's Conflict Catcher 8. This utility provides industrial-strength tools for troubleshooting software conflicts, helping you determine which parts of your system are fighting with others. Conflict Catcher provides loads of information on extensions, control panels, plug-ins, and other software add-ons, and helps you know when those items need to be upgraded (it even helps you contact the companies that produce the problem software). You can also use Conflict Catcher to prepare a detailed report on your hardware and software configuration— information that is essential for troubleshooting your system.

- *Antivirus software*—There are boogeymen in those woods—people who get their jollies by writing software (called *viruses*) that undermines and destroys the computers of strangers. Because you need to share software, you must protect yourself from these viruses. Several products that provide protection are available:

- Symantec's Norton Antivirus for Macintosh 4.0

- Dr. Solomon's Virex 5.9

- Disinfectant (a shareware program)

- *The iMac Software Restore and Software Install startup CD-ROMs*—The iMac comes with a special CD-ROM called Software Restore that you can use to boot your computer and rebuild the iMac system. If you want to add software, such as Disk First Aid, Disk Copy, or Disk Setup, use the iMac Software Install CD-ROM also included with the iMac.

 Tip   To start up from a CD-ROM, press **C** during startup.

I suggest that you obtain all these tools as soon as you can. When you have a problem that you need to solve, you don't want to have to obtain—and learn to use—new software at the same time.

DEALING WITH THE PROBLEM

Mac OS 8.5 introduces a diagnosis and repair solution that smoothes out what used to be a frustrating experience: system crashes. With Mac OS 8.5, the first thing you do when your iMac crashes is restart it. Mac OS 8.5 takes over the diagnosis and repair of common hard disk problems by running Disk First Aid during startup.

To restart a crashed Mac, do one of two things:

- Press ⌘+Control+Power key.

- Press the Restart button on the side or front of your computer.

Disk First Aid is initialized any time you use these methods to shut down and restart your Mac. Disk First Aid verifies the status of your iMac and repairs any hard disk errors it encounters. You receive no information about what was performed or discovered; your iMac just checks itself.

Problems You Might Encounter

There are several general categories of problems you may encounter:

- *Software problems*—One of the most common problems on an iMac are system extension conflicts. Another very common (and preventable problem) is that application software does not follow Apple guidelines and treads where it is not supposed to. A third possible software issue is viruses.

- *User error*—Hey, we all make mistakes. Sometimes you cause your own troubles by not properly using the tools you have (for example, installing hardware using the same SCSI ID for two separate devices), or by not following instructions (for example, installing new software without turning off your virus protection). User errors are among the most common kind; fortunately, these problems are also among the easiest to solve.

- *Hardware problems*—Sometimes, hardware fails. Hardware failures can be caused by something you do, such as installing an upgrade, or they can happen when a piece of hardware wears out. Hardware failures can be very expensive to resolve, but fortunately most hardware is very reliable. You aren't likely to have trouble in this area.

Resolving Software Problems

The bulk of your troubleshooting efforts for software problems are prevention of future problems rather than treatment of problems that have occurred. Unfortunately, software problems are unpredictable, and when they happen, there isn't usually much you can do to recover from them. You simply save and restore as much of your data as you can, reboot your machine, and begin the task of figuring out how to prevent future occurrences of the problem. If your application is acting up, save your work and begin preventive troubleshooting as soon as you can.

There are a lot of symptoms that indicate a software problem, but they usually fall into one of the following kinds of behaviors:

- Quits

- Hangs

- General misbehavior

These behaviors are typically the result of software conflicts, buggy applications, or viruses.

QUITS

Sometimes, the application you are using suddenly quits; occasionally, this quit is accompanied by an error message that tells you absolutely nothing useful. When an application quits unexpectedly, there isn't much you can do about it. It's gone. Sometimes, you can recover your data, and sometimes you can't.

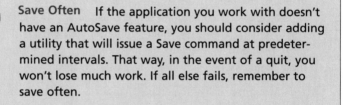

Save Often   If the application you work with doesn't have an AutoSave feature, you should consider adding a utility that will issue a Save command at predetermined intervals. That way, in the event of a quit, you won't lose much work. If all else fails, remember to save often.

HANGS

Sometimes software errors cause your application—or iMac—to freeze or hang. When this happens, your machine seems to lock up and you won't even be able to make the pointer move onscreen. Again, when this happens, you lose all the changes that you made to the open document since the last time that you saved it.

When an application hangs, you can attempt a *force quit*:

1. Press ⌘+Option+Esc.

2. Click Force Quit in the dialog box that opens.

3. The iMac attempts to shut down the problem application.

4. If it works, you are returned to the desktop.

5. Immediately save all the work in other open applications and restart your iMac.

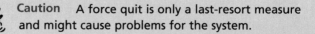

Caution   A force quit is only a last-resort measure and might cause problems for the system.

If the force quit doesn't work, you need to reboot your iMac by pressing
⌘+Control+Power key. You should use this method only when left with
no alternative.

BATTLING SOFTWARE CONFLICTS

Often, the root of a software problem lies in a software conflict. The more
extensions, control panels, and applications that you use, the more likely it
is that some of this software will conflict. Conflicting software might
cause you to experience any of the following:

- Startup errors

- Quits

- Hangs

- Performance problems

The most likely source of conflicts are extensions and control panels, but
applications can occasionally conflict with each other as well.

> **Checking for Conflicts**   Known conflicts are often
> listed in Read Me files and on Web sites for software
> you install. It is a good idea to check these sources for
> known conflicts before purchasing or installing new
> software.

ISOLATING EXTENSION CONFLICTS

The basic technique to root out extension and control panel conflicts is to
systematically remove items until the problem goes away, and then return
the removed items until the problem recurs. The last item added back to
the system is the likely source of the conflict.

The primary tool for detecting these conflicts is Apple's Extensions
Manager, which enables you to turn various extensions, control panels,
and other items off or on. You can also save sets of these items, so recon-
figuring your system is simply a matter of selecting the appropriate
Extensions Manager set.

Follow these steps to use Extensions Manager to find the software that is causing conflicts:

1. Choose Extensions Manager from the Control Panels folder from the Apple menu. Extensions Manager opens (see Figure 17.1).

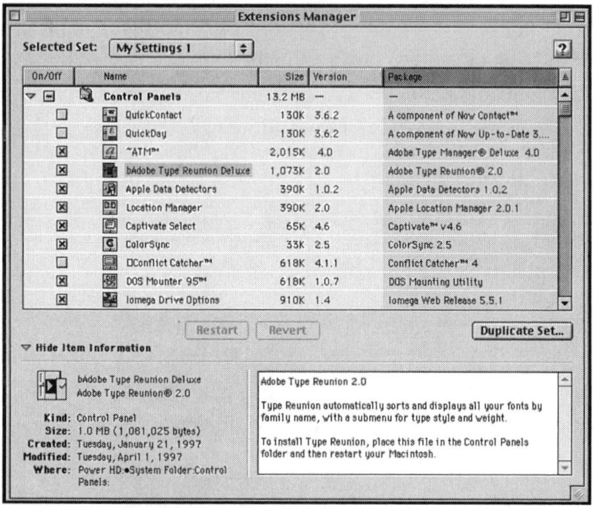

FIGURE 17.1   Extensions Manager in action.

2. Choose New Set from the File menu.

3. Type a name for your set (try something such as Set1), and click OK.

4. Scroll through the lists of control panels, extensions, and other items, clicking the On/Off check boxes for those that might be related to your problems. Continue this process until you have turned off about half of the items.

> **Narrow It Down**   Try to focus on items that are related to the application or function you were using at the time of the problem. For example, if you were trying to connect with your modem, choose the items that are related to that activity.

5. Restart your computer.

6. Try to duplicate the problem. If it doesn't happen again, you can probably assume that the problem item is one that you turned off.

7. Go back to Extensions Manager and turn on about half of those items that you turned off. Save this group of settings.

8. Restart the computer to see whether the problem happens again. If it doesn't happen, you know the problem isn't caused by one of the items you turned back on, and that the culprit is still off.

9. Repeat steps 7 and 8 until the problem happens again.

After the problem happens again, you know that the conflicting software is in the group you just turned on. Simply continue turning items off and on, narrowing the groups down until you are left with a single item that proves to be the culprit.

Eventually you will identify the software that is causing the problem. When you do, you can do one of the following:

- *Live without it*—If you can do without the problem software, you can solve the problem by leaving the item off.

- *Get an upgrade*—You can try to get an upgrade for the item to see if the conflict has been solved.

- *Change the loading order*—You can rename items to change the order in which they load into the system. Sometimes conflicts can be eliminated by changing the loading order.

DETECTING BUGGY APPLICATIONS

If you have plenty of RAM and no conflicts or other system-level problems, but your system still quits, hangs, or otherwise misbehaves, it might just be that the application is buggy. In the case of a buggy application, the only real solution is to get a bug fix release of the application (assuming that the publisher will issue one). You might have to live with the problem. If it conflicts with another application you also need, one of them might have to go. The bottom line is that there are some things you won't be able to fix. If an application is flawed, there probably isn't much you can do about it.

DETECTING VIRUSES

Viruses can cause software problems for you, including quits, hangs, or poor performance. You should suspect a virus if something particularly strange is happening, such as

- Weird messages

- The appearance of strange dialog boxes

- Persistent crashes

If a virus does infest your machine, you will need to use an antivirus tool such as Symantec Norton Antivirus for Macintosh or Dr. Solomon's Virex 5.8. These applications have features that can identify and eliminate viruses from your machine (see Figure 17.2).

FIGURE 17.2 Fighting viruses with Virex.

RESOLVING HARDWARE PROBLEMS

Although many hardware failures require a trip to a service technician, there are several hardware problems that you can troubleshoot and fix on your own. When you have a hardware problem, start simple:

- Always try a simple reboot before taking any more drastic measures.

- Check all the cables that connect various components to your system. Turn the power off, and check each cable to make sure that it is properly plugged in. Sometimes a loose cable prevents the system from operating properly.

- Strip the system down to its basic components. Disconnect everything except what you need to start the machine. If the machine boots in the stripped condition, you know that the problem lies in one of the peripherals. If the machine still doesn't boot, you know that the machine is the problem.

If these efforts fail, you'll have to take more drastic measures.

ZAPPING THE PRAM

If you're having problems with your date and system preferences, try zapping the PRAM. Parameter RAM (PRAM) is an area of your iMac that stores the information that needs to be retained when the power to the computer is turned off. These settings include time and date, system preferences, and so on. Occasionally, your iMac will start acting oddly and will seem to lose its mind every time you restart it.

To zap the PRAM using the keyboard, hold down ⌘+Option+P+R while you restart your Mac. When it starts back up, the PRAM will be cleared. Then you will have to reset the date and time as well as all your other custom settings.

 If You Lose Your Settings   Note that if you zap the PRAM, you will lose all your system settings and will have to reconfigure everything that you changed from the defaults.

REPAIRING THE HARD DISK

As you use your disk drive, the constant writing and reading of data to the drive can lead to the data structure of the disk becoming corrupted. When this happens, the disk might not mount—or if it does, you might get disk errors when you try to write data to it.

You can use a variety of tools to check and repair a disk's data structure, including Apple Disk First Aid, which comes with the iMac, or a third-party tool such as Norton Utilities or MicroMat TechTools 2.0. To use Norton to check and repair a disk, do the following:

1. Launch Norton Utilities.

2. Click the Norton Disk Doctor button.

3. In the Disk Doctor window, select a disk to check and repair.

4. Click the Examine button. You will see a progress window as the good doctor checks your drive.

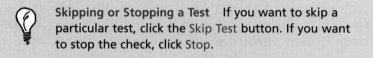

Skipping or Stopping a Test   If you want to skip a particular test, click the Skip Test button. If you want to stop the check, click Stop.

5. As problems are found, various dialog boxes tell you what the problems are and ask if you want to fix them. You should choose to fix all the errors that the Disk Doctor finds. Don't be shocked if you see numerous problem dialog boxes. There will often be several.

6. When you reach the end of the tests, you will see a Clipboard showing the results of your checkup. Click Show Report to see the details of the problems found and the repairs made to your disk. If you don't want to see the details, click Done.

After Norton finishes repairing your drive, you should notice fewer problems with it. Sometimes these repairs can have very dramatic results, and will make a non-mountable disk mountable. Other times, you might not notice much difference. It just depends on how bad the errors on your disk are.

Making Repairs with Norton   Note that you will need to boot from the Norton CD-ROM in order to fix problems on the disk that has the active system software on it. In other words, keep a version of Norton on the original CD-ROM so that you can repair straight from the CD-ROM if need be.

In this chapter, you learned to troubleshoot your system and resolve various types of problems, including hardware and software problems.

INDEX

E

J-K